ENGLISH CIVIL WAR FLAGS

The English & Scottish Foot Regiments

A Redcrest Publication

Text and flag illustrations by Steve Archibald

ISBN: 978-1-9996677-1-9

Redcrest Publishing
9 Chalfont Close, Hemel Hempstead, Herts. HP2 7JR

Black and white illustration credits: Page 3, Artist unknown *(Cassell's History of England Vol 3, 1909)*. Page 4, Ernest Crofts *(Cassell's History of England Vol 3, 1865)*. Page 9, Thomas Henry Nicholson *(Cassell's History of England, 1865)*. Page 26, Jacob de Gheyn (II) *(Instructions for the use of the musket, 1607)*. Page 35, Ernest Crofts *(Cassell's Illustrated Universal History, 1882)*. Title page and front cover illustrations by the author.

Introduction

The aim of this book is to produce a collection of as many foot regiment flags from the Civil War with as little speculation as possible. Using a variety of sources including drawings and fairly detailed descriptions from the time plus some current material I have illustrated as many as I could whilst being fairly confident they are as accurate as they can be.

Of course the civil war lasted many years and regiments were formed, merged and disbanded and the relatively small collection I have illustrated are only snapshots of the period. I hope this book will prove to be a handy resource of all the known flags for historians, wargamers and battle re-enactors.

The main references I used to compile these illustrations include the first hand records from Richard Symonds' Notebook and Dairy, Jonathon Turmile's notes, Levet and Lucas' observations of London Trained Bands, and Fitzpayne Fisher's detailed records of Scottish flags. I also referred to more recent publications including 'The English Emblem Tradition Volume 3' edited by Alan R Young and ECW Flags and Colours by Peachy & Prince and many more.

Parliamentarian 'Roundhead' troops

Contents

Fight for the Standard at the Battle of Edge Hill

Heraldry in ECW Flags

In general flags during this period seemed to follow the main rules of heraldry. This included using mainly simple heraldic devices in a 'metal' either yellow (gold) or white (silver) on a coloured field and vice versa. Other devices appeared as elements from a coat of of arms, usually from the regiments commander. The colours used were mostly the basic heraldic ones although there are recorded instances of others such as a pale green blue (watchet).

HERALDIC COLOURS

	ENGLISH	HERALDIC NAME
METAL	Yellow or Gold	Or
	White or Silver	Argent
COLOUR	Red	Gules
	Blue	Azure
	Green	Vert
	Black	Sable
	Purple	Purpure
	Orange/Tawny	Tenne
	Crimson	Sanguine of Murrey

COMMON HERALDIC DEVICES

ENGLISH	HERALDIC NAME
1. Piles	Piles
2. Stream Blazant	Piles Wavy
3. Stars	Mullets
4. Discs	Torteaux (Red), Plates (White), Hurts (Blue), Pommels (Green), Gunstones (Black), Golpes (Purple), Oranges (Orange)
5. Diamonds	Lozenges or Fusils
6. Crosses	Crosses
7. Rectangles	Billets
8. Crescents	Crescents
9. Arrow Heads	Pheon or Feon

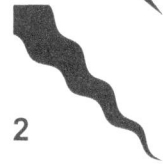

1

2

3

4

5

6

7

8

9

5

Regimental Identification Systems

There are believed to be two main regimental flag systems in use during the English Civil Wars. One described by Captain Thomas Venn "The Colonels Colours in the first place is of a pure and clean colour, without any mixture. The Lieutenant Colonel's only with Saint Georges Cross in the upper corner next the staff; the Major's the same; but in the lower and outermost corner with a little stream blazant (pile wavy), and every Captain with a Saint Georges Armes alone, but with so many spots or several devices as partain to the dignity of their respective places."

The second system followed along the

SYSTEM A

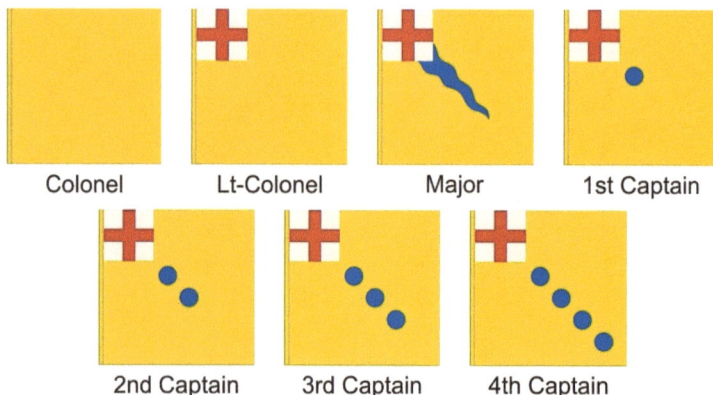

| Colonel | Lt-Colonel | Major | 1st Captain |

| 2nd Captain | 3rd Captain | 4th Captain |

SYSTEM B

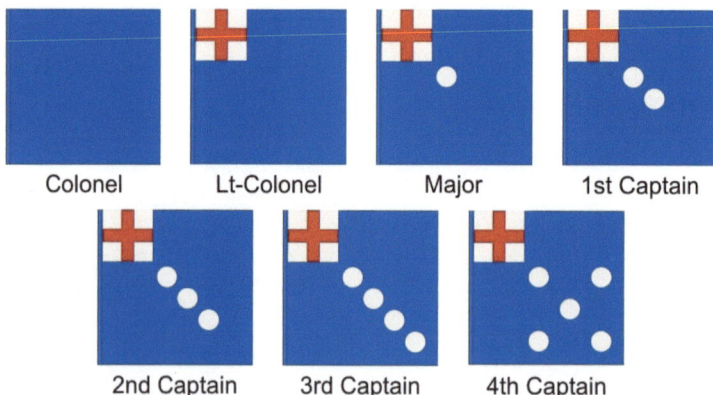

| Colonel | Lt-Colonel | Major | 1st Captain |

| 2nd Captain | 3rd Captain | 4th Captain |

same lines but the Major's pile wavy was replaced by the single dot or device, meaning that the flag with two dots or devices became the 1st Captains, three dots 2nd Captains, etc. This makes identifying which flag belonged to which Captain impossible for some regiments unless you have a drawing or description that the Major's flag carried a pile wavy.

A slight variation of this 2nd system appeared with some Trained Bands and possibly Colonel Thelwel's regiments that only used a number piles and piles wavy instead of the devices.

With all these systems though you will see from the examples in this book that slight deviations and anomalies occur sometimes - there was a war going on after all.

One system which appeared to be very rare was a gyronny type which used the number of 'pie' slices to differentiate the Captain's company. It only appeared on a handful of Royalist units and is thought be linked to an Irish expedition or maybe

PILEY SYSTEM

| Colonel | Lt-Colonel | Major | 1st Captain |

| 2nd Captain | 3rd Captain | 4th Captain |

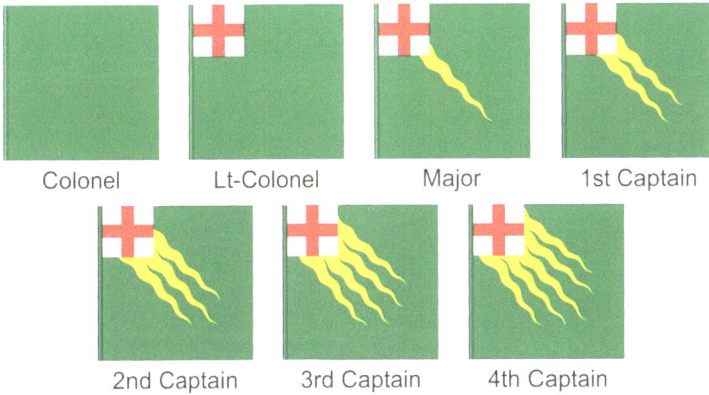

GYRONNY SYSTEM

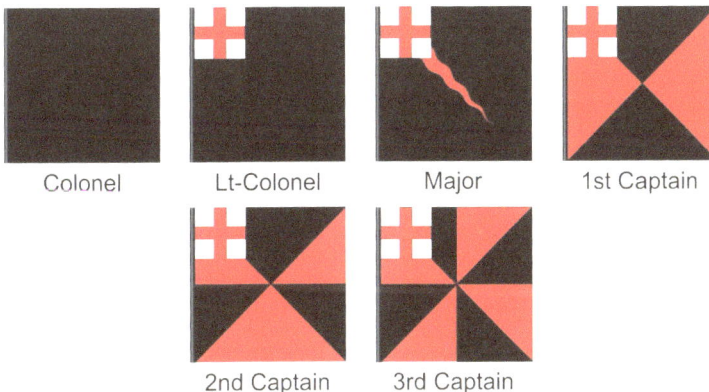

| Colonel | Lt-Colonel | Major | 1st Captain |

| 2nd Captain | 3rd Captain |

7

SCOTTISH SYSTEM

Colonel

1st Captain

3rd Captain

4th Captain

foreign troops from a sympathetic European king.

There are a very few documented examples of stripy flags of various colours and numbers of stripes. It is thought that they might be from an earlier system before the civil war. Maybe they could have been brought out of mothballs for a hurriedly assembled regiment.

One final mention has to be for the flamboyant Prince Rupert's regimental colours, a system that will keep historians busy for decades trying to work it out. Is it the number of slices or rings that identify the unit? (see page 22).

The Scottish organisation of a regiment was same as the English but the system of identification was slightly different. The Colonels flag was nearly always white and usually displayed the colonel's personal device, crest or motto along with the Covenant motto. All other units carried the saltire either as the full flag or occasionally as a cantire in the top next to the staff. The colours of the saltires varied

with red and blue with white cross being the most popular. The Covenant motto was carried on (nearly) all flags although the the actual words and spelling varied.

There were three main ways the individual companies were identified. The simplest of these was to use numbers of devices in the centre of the cross, for example 4 stars was the 4th Captain's colour. Second type was heraldic cadency devices to identify the different Captain's companies. Originally these cadency devices were placed on a coat of arms to identify a 1st, 2nd, 3rd, etc, son or daughter. The illustration on this page shows devices and their meaning.

This wasn't very popular though as many seem to have the numbers painted next to the device. Maybe because the lower ranks were not very familiar with the gentries rules of heraldry.

The final type was using emblems and mottos in the centre of the cross, which would have meant that only the members of that unit knew which flag to rally to.

CADENCY DEVICES

1st

2nd

3rd

4th

5th

6th

A mortally wounded Colonel John Hampden is helped from the Chalgrove battlefield.

Royalist Foot Regiments

Additional Notes To Illustrations

R2-R10. A number of King's Lifeguard colours captured at the Battle of Naseby 1645

R11-R15 and R17-R20. Two sets of Sir Henry Bard's colours taken a year apart.

R16. Sir Charles Gerrard's colours are described as azure (blue) and filmont (an orangey brown). The origin of the gold laurel is unclear, maybe company distinction award. Another flag from this regiment was plain blue.

R24-R26. The red distinction on Bernard Ashley's colours are a bit of a mystery. It might represent a fishing lure or a bomb.

R39-R43. Sir Gilbert Talbot's colours featured a black dog. Talbot is the heraldic name for a dog.

R44-R48. An complete example of the rare 'Gyronny' system on Sir Allan Apsley's Regimental colours.

R49-R54. A standard set of flags for Sir James Pennyman's Regiment except for the one with two wavy piles - the meaning of which is unknown.

R61-R66. The City of Oxford Regiment featured the lion crest from the cities coat of arms as its device. The gold peppered with blue fleurs-de-lis lion was a unique crest granted to the city by Queen Elizabeth I. It holds the Tudor Rose and wears the Royal Crown. Correctly, though, the lion should be guardant with its head facing the viewer and not passant (looking left). However I have illustrated them here as the artist (R Symonds who sketched them at the time) has drawn them passant. The motto on the Lieutenant-Colonel's flag is also from the coat of arms.

R69-R72. Prince Rupert's Regiment carried a unique system of company identification. Unfortunately the meaning of the combination of black, white and blue-grey piles and black rings (annulets) is totally unknown.

R73-R76. An unknown regiment believed to be attached to Prince Rupert at Naseby. The Colonel's flag depicts a white borage plant with the other company devices as white stars.

R81-R82. Two examples of the 'old' stripey identification system from two unknown units.

R85. Another example of the mysterious fishing lure/bomb device.

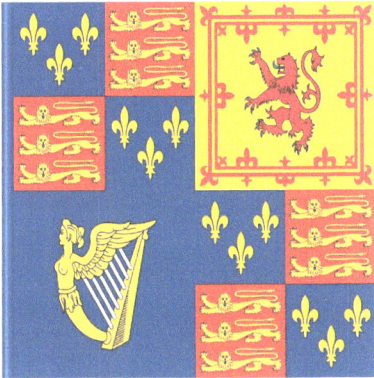

R1. The Stuart Royal Standard

R2. The King's Lifeguard
Colonel's colour. Naseby 1645

R3. The King's Lifeguard
Lt Colonel's colour. Naseby 1645

R4. The King's Lifeguard
Major's colour. Naseby 1645

R5. The King's Lifeguard
1st Captain's colour. Naseby 1645

R6 The King's Lifeguard
2nd Captain's colour. Naseby 1645

R7. The King's Lifeguard
3rd Captain's colour. Naseby 1645

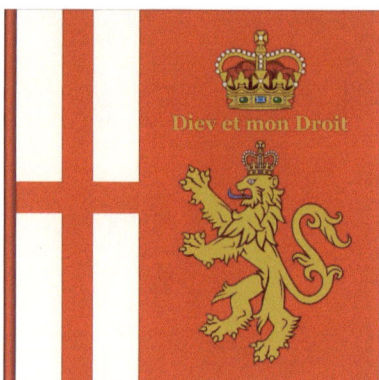

R8. The King's Lifeguard
Unidentified colour. Naseby 1645

R9. The King's Lifeguard
Unidentified colour. Naseby 1645

R10. The King's Lifeguard
Unidentified colour. Naseby 1645

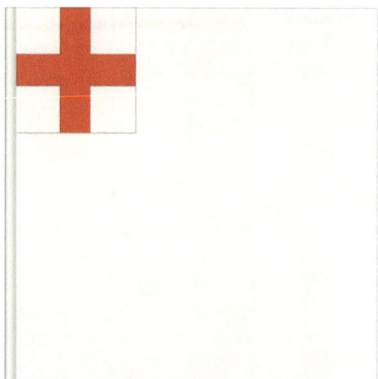

R11. Sir Henry Bard's Regiment
Lt Colonel's colour. Aldbourne 1644

R12. Sir Henry Bard's Regiment
Major's colour. Aldbourne 1644

R13. Sir Henry Bard's Regiment
1st Captain's colour. Aldbourne 1644

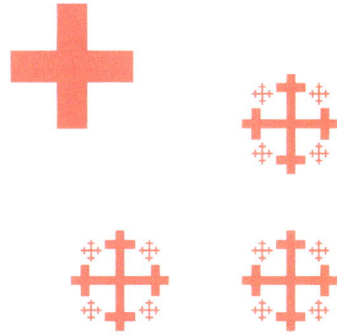

R14. Sir Henry Bard's Regiment
2nd Captain's colour. Aldbourne 1644

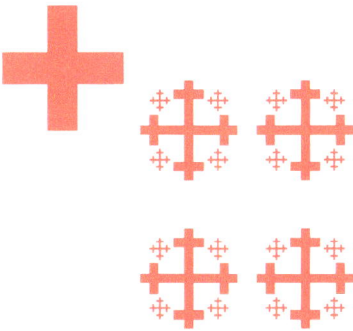

R15. Sir Henry Bard's Regiment
3rd Captain's colour. Aldbourne 1644

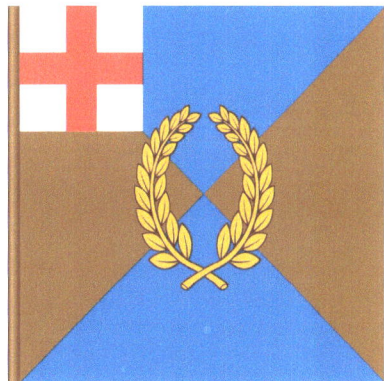

R16. Sir Charles Gerard's Regiment
Aldbourne 1644

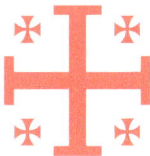

R17. Sir Henry Bard's Regiment
Lt Colonel's colour. Naseby 1645

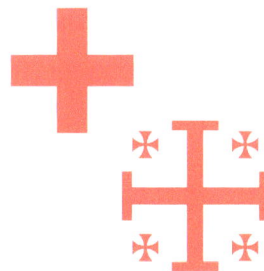

R18. Sir Henry Bard's Regiment
Major's colour. Naseby 1645

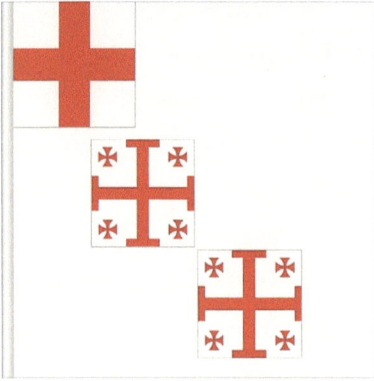

R19. Sir Henry Bard's Regiment
1st Captain's colour. Naseby 1645

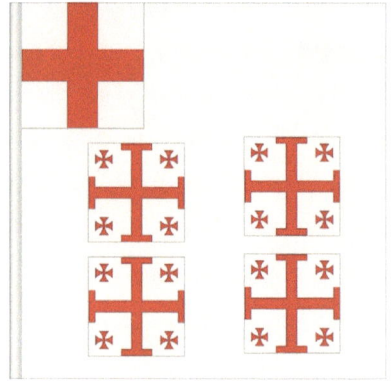

R20. Sir Henry Bard's Regiment
3rd Captain's colour. Naseby 1645

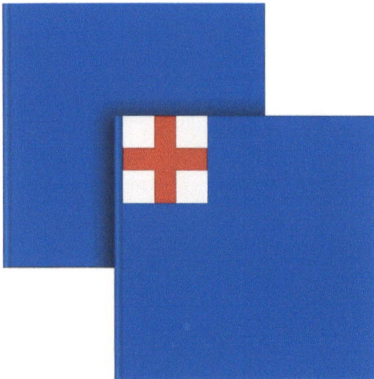

R21. Colonel Anthony Thelwel's Regiment
Colonel and Lt Colonel's colour.
Aldbourne 1644

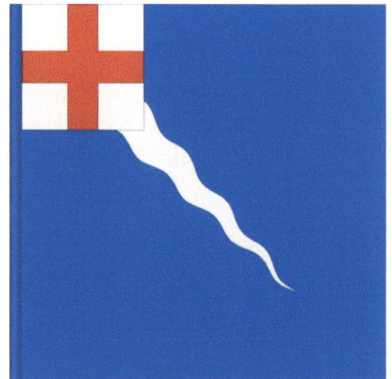

R22. Colonel Anthony Thelwel's Regiment
Major's colour. Aldbourne 1644

R23. Colonel Anthony Thelwel's Regiment
1st Captains colour. Aldbourne 1644

R24. Sir Arthur Aston's Regiment
1st or 2nd Captains colour

R25. Colonel Bernard Ashley's Regiment
Colonel & Lt Colonel's colour.
Aldbourne 1644

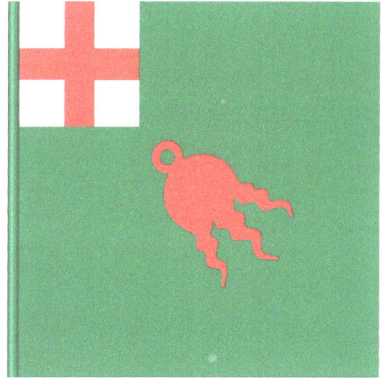

R26. Colonel Bernard Ashley's Regiment
Major's colour.
Aldbourne 1644

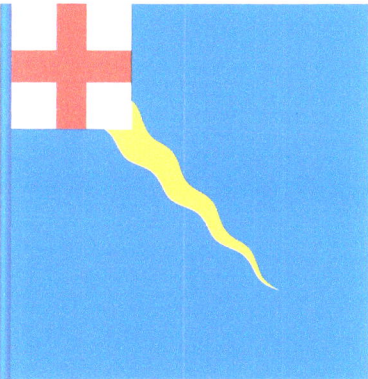

R27. Colonel Richard Bagot's Regiment
Major's colour. 1645

R28. Colonel Richard Bagot's Regiment
1st Captains colour. 1645

R29. Colonel Richard Bagot's Regiment
2nd Captains colour. 1645

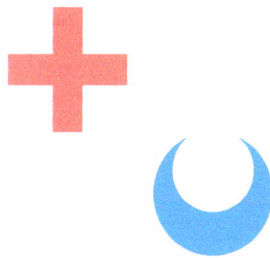

R30. Col Henry Lord Percy's Regiment
Major's colour. Aldbourne 1644

R31. Col Sir Lewis Dyve's Regiment
Colonel & Lt Colonel's colour.
Aldbourne 1644

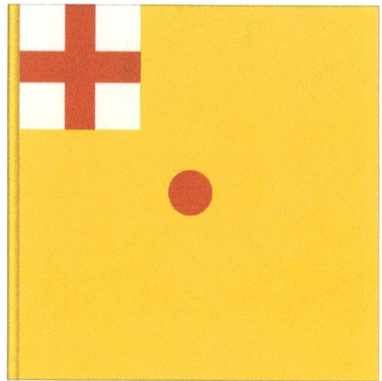

R32. Col Sir Lewis Dyve's Regiment
Major's colour.
Aldbourne 1644

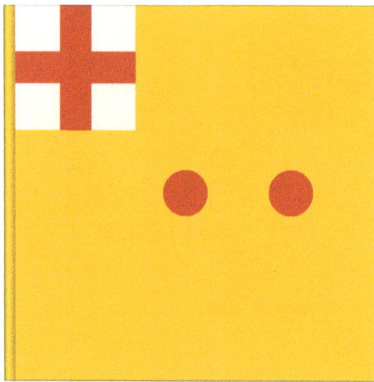

R33. Col Sir Lewis Dyve's Regiment
1st Captain's colour.
Aldbourne 1644

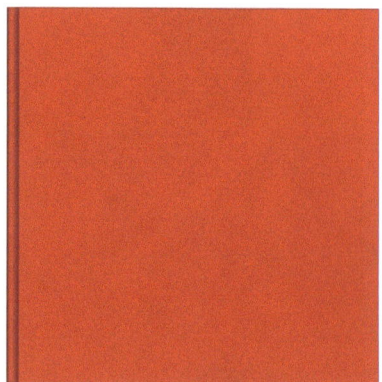

R34. Lord Ralph Hopton's Regiment
Colonel's colour.
Aldbourne 1644

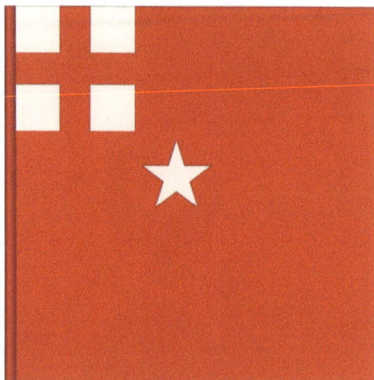

R35. Lord Ralph Hopton's Regiment
1st Captains colour.
Aldbourne 1644

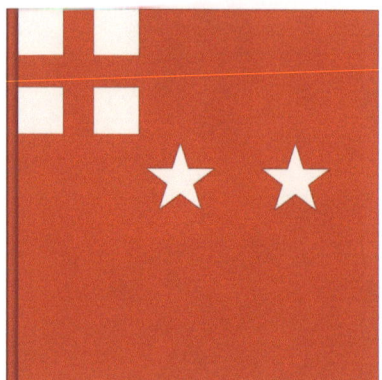

R36. Lord Ralph Hopton's Regiment
2nd Captain's colour.
Aldbourne 1644

R37. Lord Ralph Hopton's Regiment
3rd Captain's colour.
Aldbourne 1644

R38. Lord Ralph Hopton's Regiment
4th Captain's colour.
Aldbourne 1644

R39. Sir Gilbert Talbot's Regiment
Colonel & Lt Colonel's colour.
Aldbourne 1644

R40. Sir Gilbert Talbot's Regiment
Major's colour.
Aldbourne 1644

R41. Sir Gilbert Talbot's Regiment
1st Captain's colour.
Aldbourne 1644

R42. Sir Gilbert Talbot's Regiment
2nd Captain's colour.
Aldbourne 1644

R43. Sir Gilbert Talbot's Regiment
3rd Captain's colour.
Aldbourne 1644

R44. Sir Allan Apsley's Regiment
Colonel & Lt Colonel's colour.
Aldbourne 1644

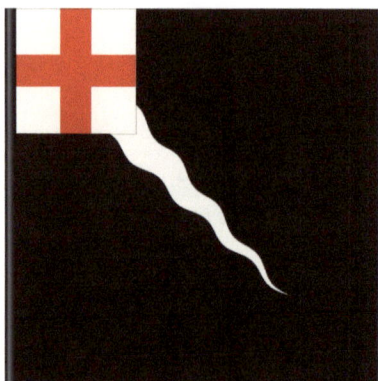

R45. Sir Allan Apsley's Regiment
Major's colour.
Aldbourne 1644

R46. Sir Allan Apsley's Regiment
1st Captain's colour.
Aldbourne 1644

R47. Sir Allan Apsley's Regiment
2nd Captain's colour.
Aldbourne 1644

R48. Sir Allan Apsley's Regiment
3rd Captain's colour.
Aldbourne 1644

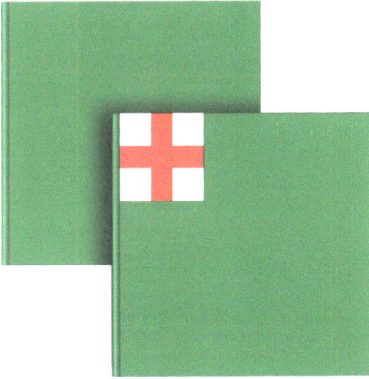

R49. Sir James Pennyman's Regiment
Colonel & Lt Colonel's colour.
Aldbourne 1644

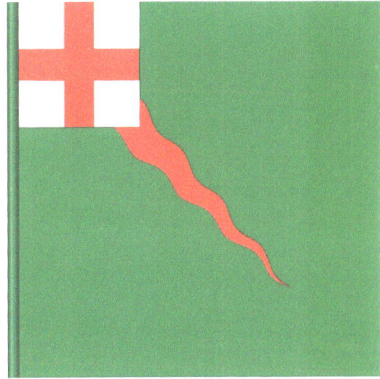

R50. Sir James Pennyman's Regiment
Major's colour.
Aldbourne 1644

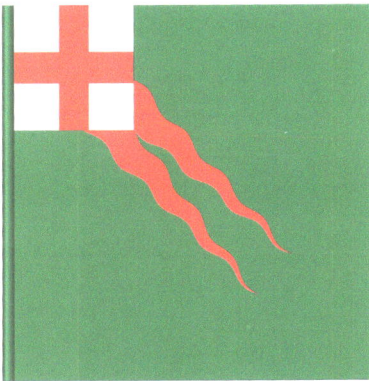

R51. Sir James Pennyman's Regiment
1st Captain's colour ?
Aldbourne 1644

R52. Sir James Pennyman's Regiment
2nd Captain's colour.
Aldbourne 1644

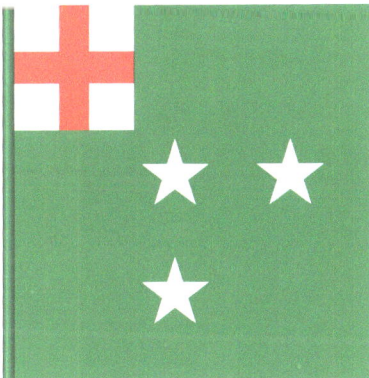

R53. Sir James Pennyman's Regiment
3rd Captain's colour.
Aldbourne 1644

R54. Sir James Pennyman's Regiment
4th Captain's colour.
Aldbourne 1644

R55. Sir Jacob Astley's Regiment
Colonel's colour. 1645

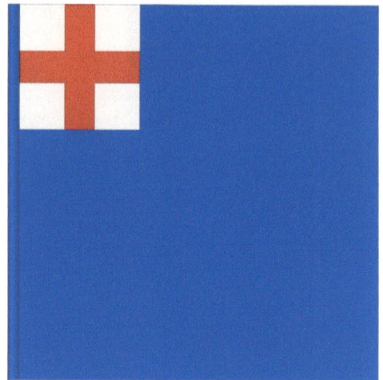
R56. Sir Jacob Astley's Regiment
Lt Colonel's colour. 1645

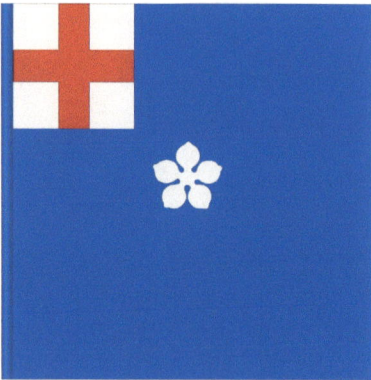
R57. Sir Jacob Astley's Regiment
Major's or 1st Captain's colour. 1645

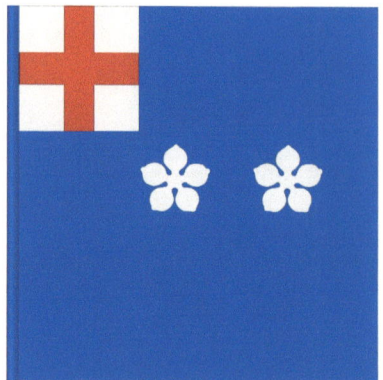
R58. Sir Jacob Astley's Regiment
1st or 2nd Captain's colour. 1645

R59. Sir Jacob Astley's Regiment
3rd or 4th Captain's colour. 1645

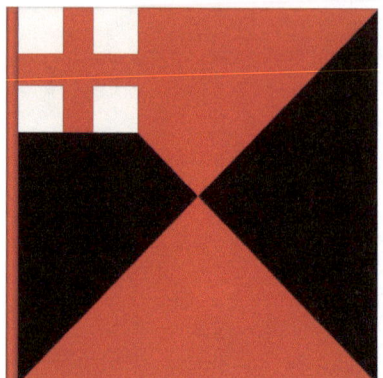
R60. Duke of York's Regiment
1st Captain's colour. Marlborough 1644

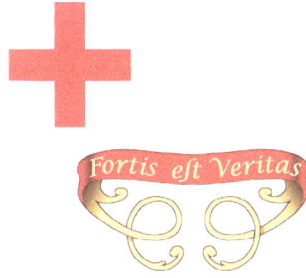

R61. City of Oxford Regiment
Colonel's colour. 1643

R62. City of Oxford Regiment
Lt Colonel's colour. 1643

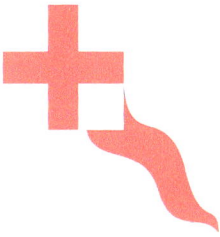

R63. City of Oxford Regiment
Sgt. Major's colour. 1643

R64. City of Oxford Regiment
1st Captain's colour. 1643

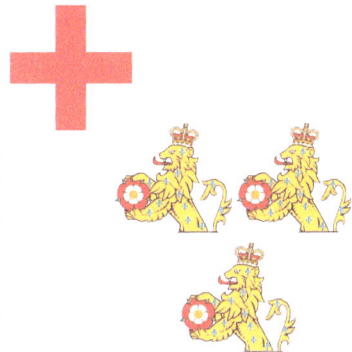

R65. City of Oxford Regiment
2nd Captain's colour. 1643

R66. City of Oxford Regiment
3rd Captain's colour. 1643

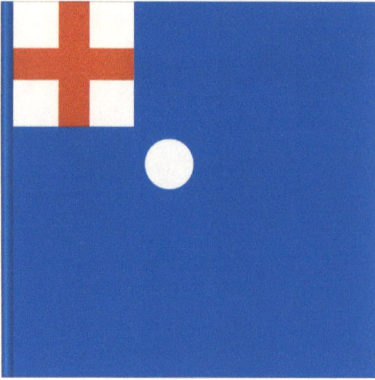

R67. Col Francis Cooke's Regiment
1st Captain's colour.
Aldbourne 1644

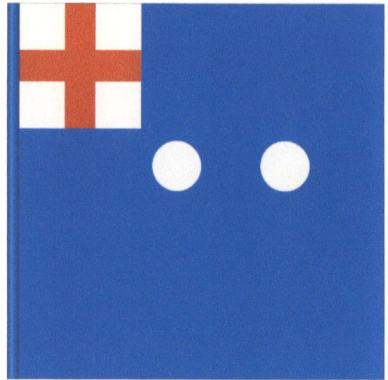

R68. Col Francis Cooke's Regiment
2nd Captain's colour.
Aldbourne 1644

R69. Prince Rupert's Regiment
Unknown colour.
Naseby. 1645

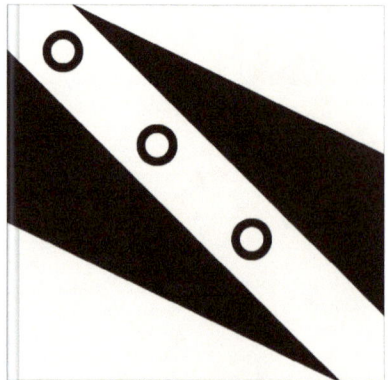

R70. Prince Rupert's Regiment
Unknown colour.
Naseby. 1645

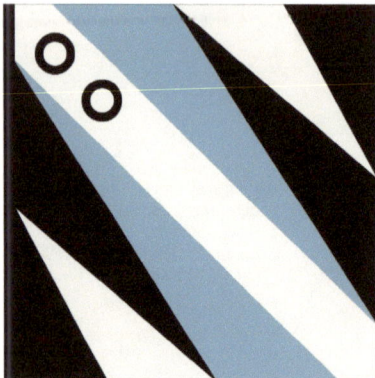

R71. Prince Rupert's Regiment
Unknown colour.
Naseby. 1645

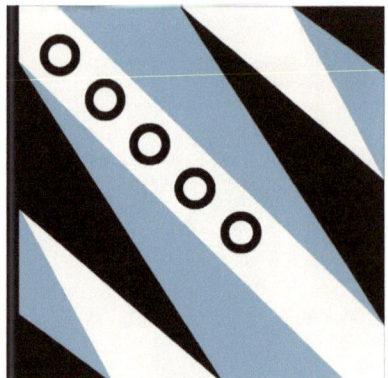

R72. Prince Rupert's Regiment
Unknown colour.
Naseby. 1645

R73. Unknown Regiment under Prince Rupert
Colonel's colour. Naseby. 1645

R74. Unknown Regiment under Prince Rupert
Lt Colonel's colour. Naseby. 1645

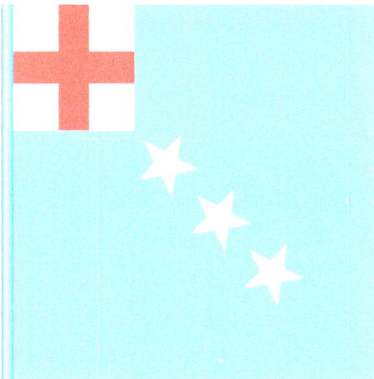

R75. Unknown Regiment under Prince Rupert. 2nd or 3rd Captain's colour. Naseby. 1645

R76. Unknown Regiment under Prince Rupert. 3rd or 4th Captain's colour. Naseby. 1645

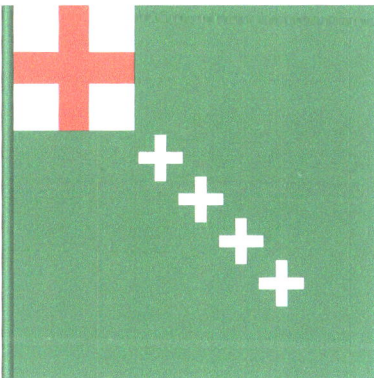

R77. Unknown Regiment
3rd or 4th Captain's colour.
Marston Moor 1644

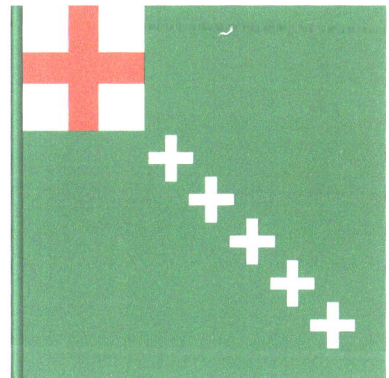

R78. Unknown Regiment
4th or 5th Captain's colour.
Marston Moor 1644

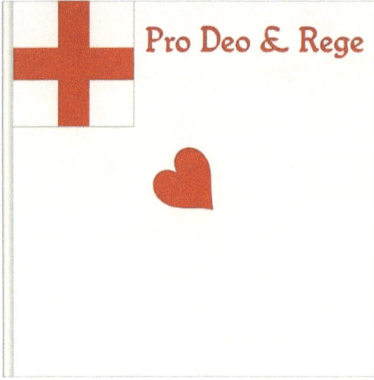

R79. Col John Taylor's Regiment
Major's or 1st Captain's colour.
Bristol 1645

R80. Col John Taylor's Regiment
1st or 2nd Captain's colour.
Bristol 1645

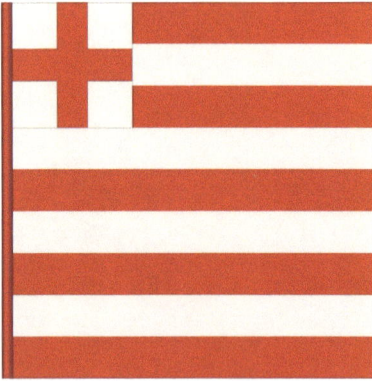

R81. Unknown Regiment
1643/44

R82. Unknown Regiment
1643/44

R83. Unknown Regiment
2nd or 3rd Captain's colour.
Maston Moor 1644

R84. Unknown Regiment
4th Captain's colour.
Maston Moor 1644

R85. Colonel Theophilius Gilby's Regiment
Major's colour. 1644

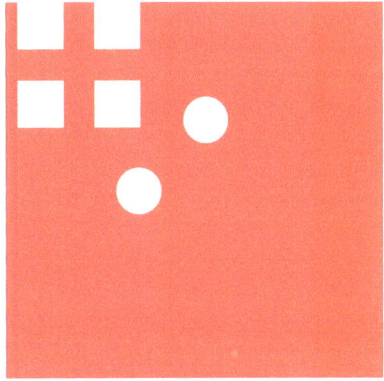

R86. Unknown Regiment
1st or 2nd Captains colour.
Edgehill 1642

R87. Unknown Regiment
Major's or 1st Captains colour.
Naseby 1645

R88. Unknown Regiment
2nd or 3rd Captains colour.
Naseby 1645

Parliamentarian Foot Regiments

Additional Notes To Illustrations

P1-P6. Earl of Essex's Regiment

P7-P16. Colonel Charles Fairfax's Regiment carried flags made of "the best taffaty of the deepest blue" with white star devices and a gold motto on the Colonel's flag.

P17-P18. The two examples of James Holbourne's flags are described as having a yellow field with tawny (a dark orange colour) devices.

P19-P22.This was originally the Lord

A typical musketeer of the period

Saye & Sele's regiment displaying the gold lion devices, Colonel Aldrich assumed command of the unit in 1643.

P23-P25. In early 1645 Colonel Aldrich's regiment were re-equipped with new flags with gold laurels replacing the gold lions.

P26. One of very few surviving examples from the period.

P27. Lord Brooke's colours are described by contemporary sources as purple. However the colour for the devices is unknown but almost certainly either white or yellow as shown.

P28. Lord Willoughby of Parham's regiment carried ensigns of "ritch watchet tafitie with distinctions of white crosses". Watchet is a light blue-green colour.

P29. Another example of a surviving flag from the period.

P30. The colours of Captain William Norris. At this time it not known which regiment he was attached to.

P31-P42. A number of regimental colours from various unknown units described in an order to a flag maker in October 1644.

P43-P44. Two flags from an unknown regiment unusually sporting gold on black mottos.

P1. Earl of Essex's Regiment
Colonel and Lt Colonel's company
Newbury 1643

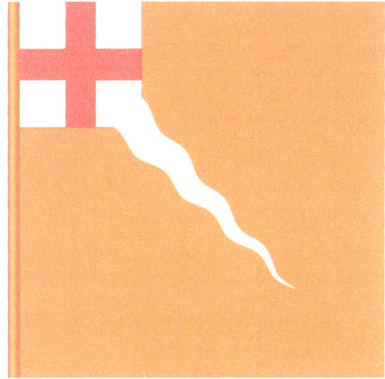

P2. Earl of Essex's Regiment
Major's company.
Newbury 1643

P3. Earl of Essex's Regiment
1st company.
Newbury 1643

P4. Earl of Essex's Regiment
2nd company.
Newbury 1643

P5. Earl of Essex's Regiment
3rd company.
Newbury 1643

P6. Earl of Essex's Regiment
4th company.
Newbury 1643

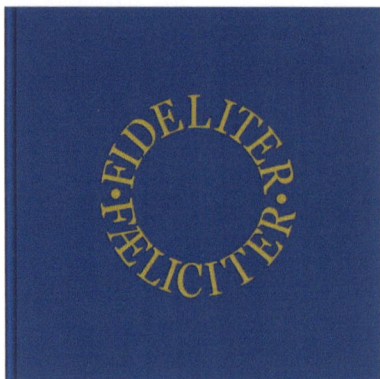

P7. Colonel Charles Fairfax's Regiment
Colonel's company 1649

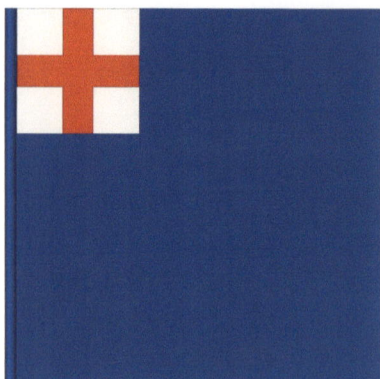

P8. Colonel Charles Fairfax's Regiment
Lt colonel's company 1649

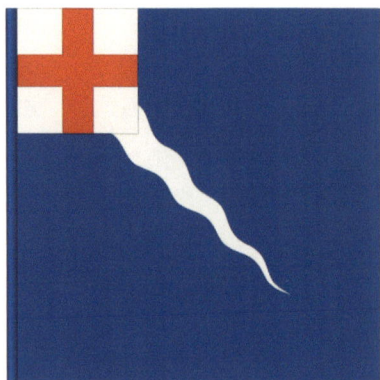

P9. Colonel Charles Fairfax's Regiment
Major's company 1649

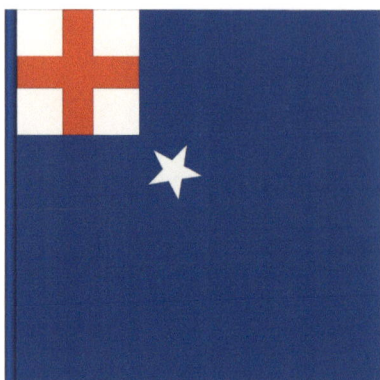

P10. Colonel Charles Fairfax's Regiment
1st company 1649

P11. Colonel Charles Fairfax's Regiment
2nd company 1649

P12. Colonel Charles Fairfax's Regiment
3rd company 1649

P13. Colonel Charles Fairfax's Regiment
4th company 1649

P14. Colonel Charles Fairfax's Regiment
5th company 1649

P15. Colonel Charles Fairfax's Regiment
6th company 1649

P16. Colonel Charles Fairfax's Regiment
7th company 1649

P17. Colonel James Holbourne's Regiment
2nd or 3rd company 1642-43

P18. Colonel James Holbourne's Regiment
4th or 5th company 1642-43

P19. Colonel Edward Aldrich's Regiment
Major's or 1st company
Before December 1644

P20. Colonel Edward Aldrich's Regiment
1st or 2nd company
Before December 1644

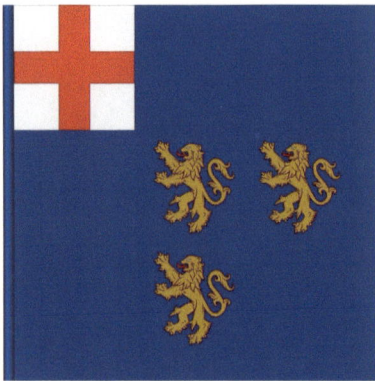

P21. Colonel Edward Aldrich's Regiment
2nd or 3rd company
Before December 1644

P22. Colonel Edward Aldrich's Regiment
3rd or 4th company
Before December 1644

P23. Colonel Edward Aldrich's Regiment
1st or 2nd company 1645

P24. Colonel Edward Aldrich's Regiment
2nd or 3rd company 1645

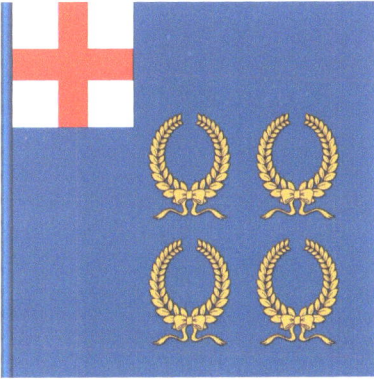

P25. Colonel Edward Aldrich's Regiment
3rd or 4th company 1645

P26. Sir John Gell's Regiment
5th company 1643-44
Surviving Example

P27. Lord Brooke's Regiment
5th company 1642

P28. Lord Willoughby of Parham's
Regiment
4th company 1643

P29. Sir Alexander Carew's Regiment
3rd or 4th company 1643
Surviving Example

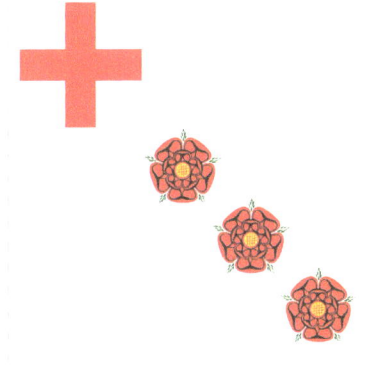

P30. Unknown Regiment
Captain William Norris' company
1642/43

P31. Unknown Regiment
1st or 2nd company 1644

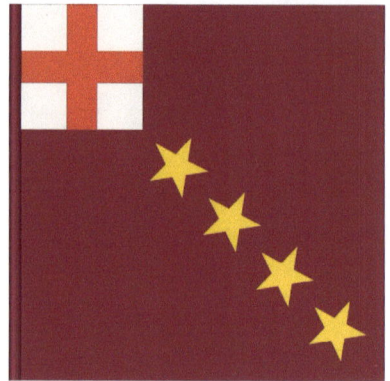

P32. Unknown Regiment
3rd or 4th company 1644

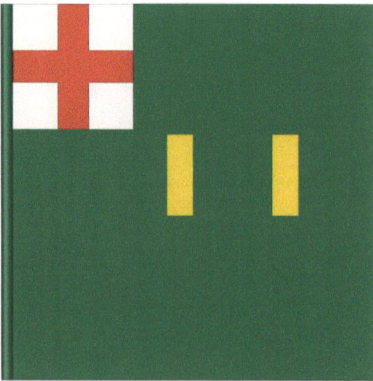

P33. Unknown Regiment
1st or 2nd company 1644

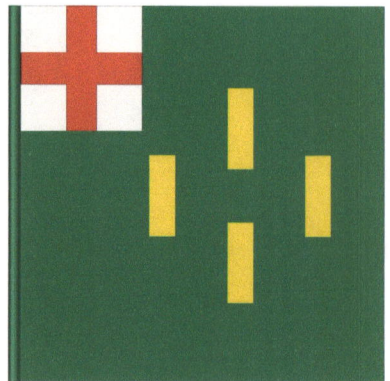

P34. Unknown Regiment
3rd or 4th company 1644

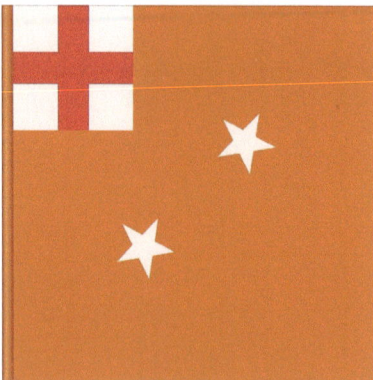

P35. Unknown Regiment
1st or 2nd company 1644

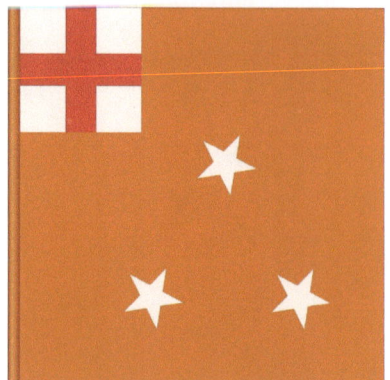

P36. Unknown Regiment
2nd or 3rd company 1644

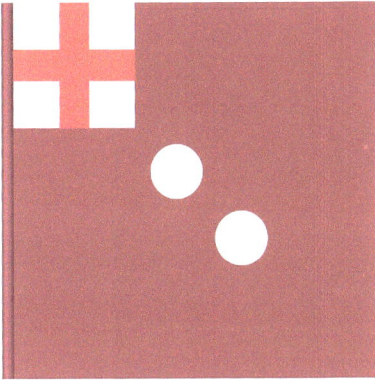

P37. Unknown Regiment
1st or 2nd company 1644

P38. Unknown Regiment
3rd or 4th company 1644

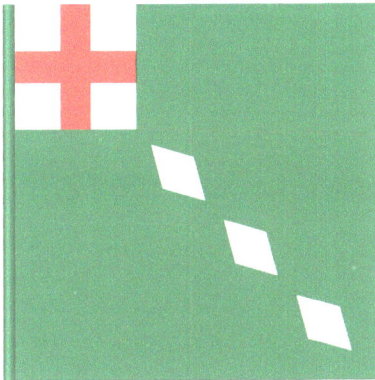

P39. Unknown Regiment
2nd or 3rd company 1644

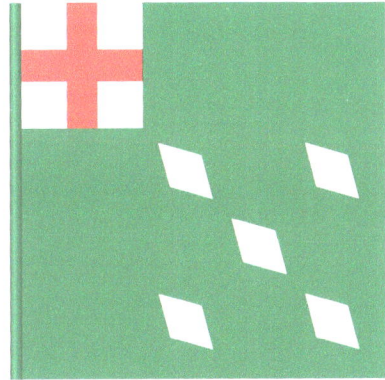

P40. Unknown Regiment
4th or 5th company 1644

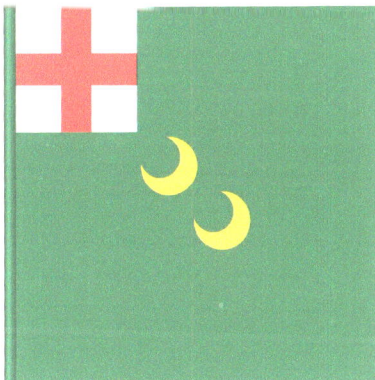

P41. Unknown Regiment
1st or 2nd company 1644

P42. Unknown Regiment
2nd or 4th company 1644

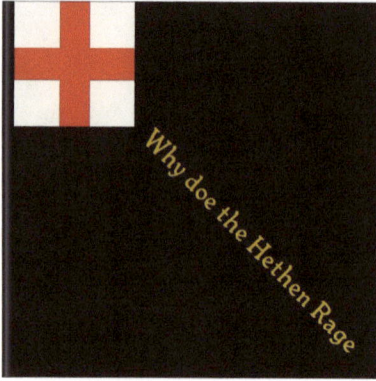

P43. Unknown Regiment
Lt Colonel's company 1642

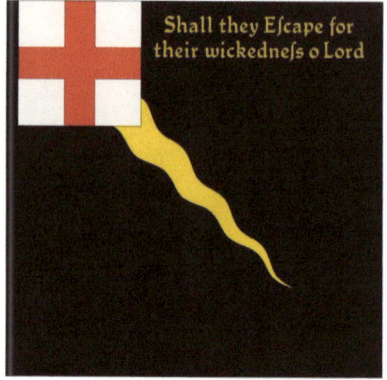

P44. Unknown Regiment
Major's company 1642

Trained Bands Foot Regiments

Additional Notes To Illustrations

The Trained Bands were local militia controlled by individual counties and were the only permanent military units in England at the outbreak of the civil wars. During the war period various Trained Bands contributed regiments to both sides of the conflict depending on their allegiance. The London Trained Bands of 1643 have been very well documented from the period and show perfect examples of the organization of a foot regiment at that time. The only exception to this was the Tower Hamlets Regiment, with motto and laurel on all flags.

The Battle of Marston Moor

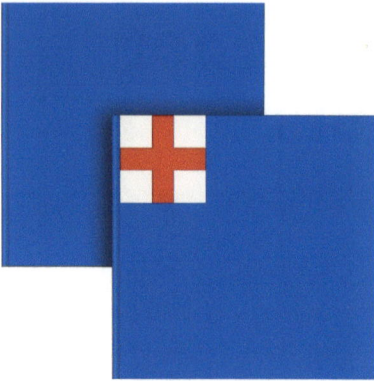

TB1. The Blew London Trayned Bands
Regiment
Colonel and Lt Colonel's colour 1643

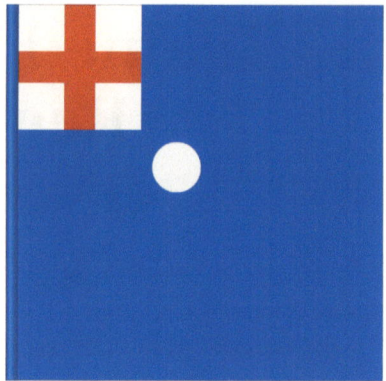

TB2. The Blew London Trayned Bands
Regiment
Major's colour 1643

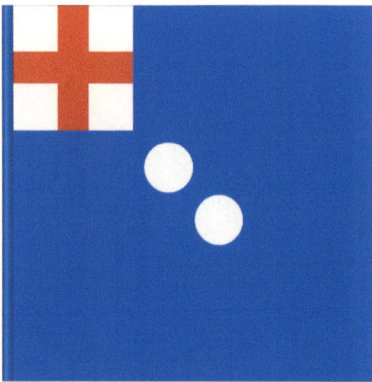

TB3. The Blew London Trayned Bands
Regiment
1st Captain's colour 1643

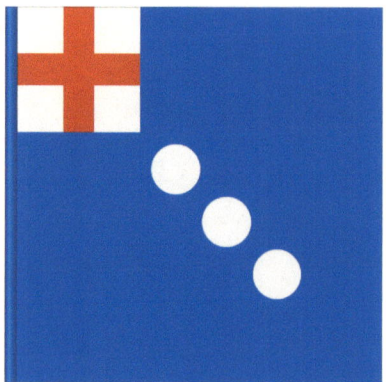

TB4. The Blew London Trayned Bands
Regiment
2nd Captain's colour 1643

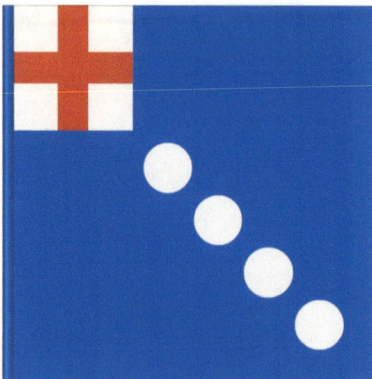

TB5. The Blew London Trayned Bands
Regiment
3rd Captain's colour 1643

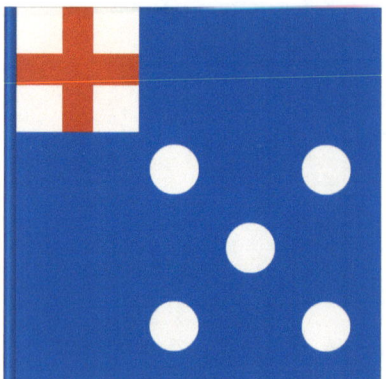

TB6. The Blew London Trayned Bands
Regiment
4th Captain's colour 1643

TB7. The Red London Trayned Bands
Regiment
Colonel and Lt Colonel's colour 1643

TB8. The Red London Trayned Bands
Regiment
Major's colour 1643

TB9. The Red London Trayned Bands
Regiment
1st Captain's colour 1643

TB10. The Red London Trayned Bands
Regiment
2nd Captain's colour 1643

TB11. The Red London Trayned Bands
Regiment
3rd Captain's colour 1643

TB12. The Red London Trayned Bands
Regiment
4th Captain's colour 1643

37

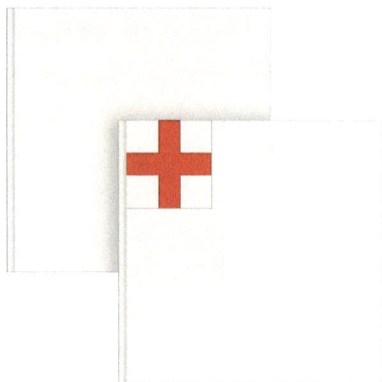

TB13. The White London Trayned Bands
Regiment
Colonel and Lt Colonel's colour 1643

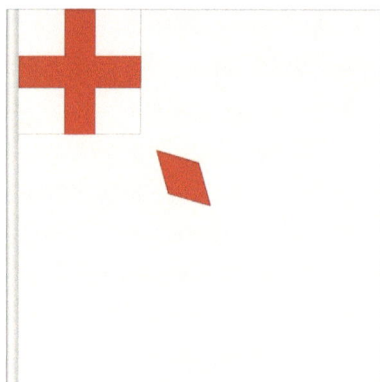

TB14. The White London Trayned Bands
Regiment
Major's colour 1643

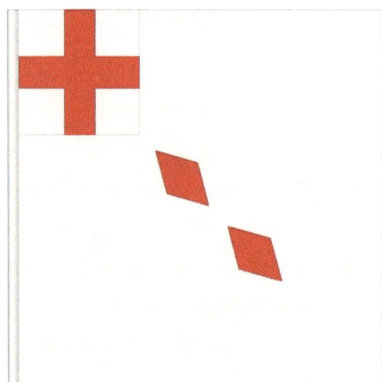

TB15. The White London Trayned Bands
Regiment
1st Captain's colour 1643

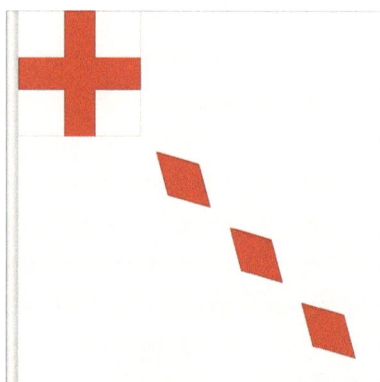

TB16. The White London Trayned Bands
Regiment
2nd Captain's colour 1643

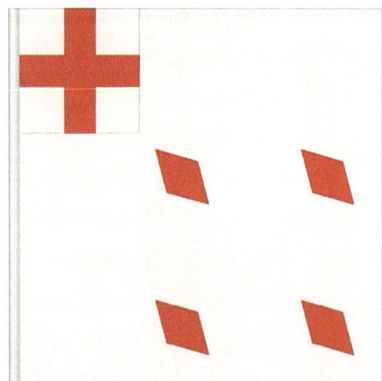

TB17. The White London Trayned Bands
Regiment
3rd Captain's colour 1643

TB18. The White London Trayned Bands
Regiment
4th Captain's colour 1643

TB19. The White London Trayned Bands
Regiment
Major's (Alternate) colour 1643

TB20. The White London Trayned Bands
Regiment
1st Captain's (Alternate) colour 1643

TB21. The White London Trayned Bands
Regiment
3rd Captain's (Alternate) colour 1643

TB22. The Yellow London Trayned Bands
Regiment
Colonel and Lt Colonel's colour 1643

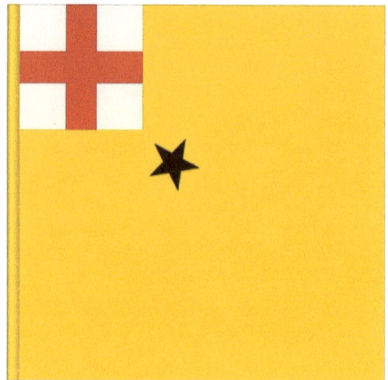

TB23. The Yellow London Trayned Bands
Regiment
Major's colour 1643

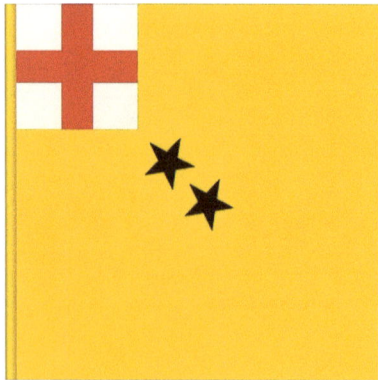

TB24. The Yellow London Trayned Bands
Regiment
1st Captain's colour 1643

TB25. The Yellow London Trayned Bands
Regiment
2nd Captain's colour 1643

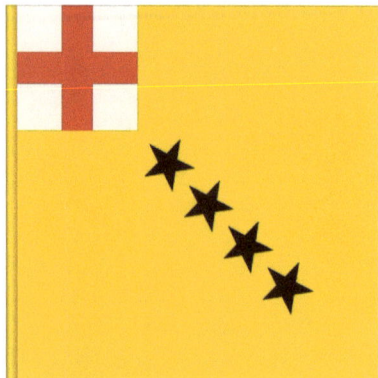

TB26. The Yellow London Trayned Bands
Regiment
3rd Captain's colour 1643

TB27. The Yellow London Trayned Bands
Regiment
4th Captain's colour 1643

TB28. The Yellow London Trayned Bands
Regiment
2nd Captain's (Alternate) colour 1643

TB29. The Yellow London Trayned Bands
Regiment
4th Captain's (Alternate) colour 1643

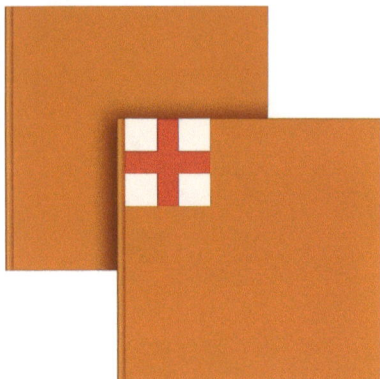

TB30. The Orange London Trayned Bands
Regiment
Colonel and Lt Colonel's colour 1643

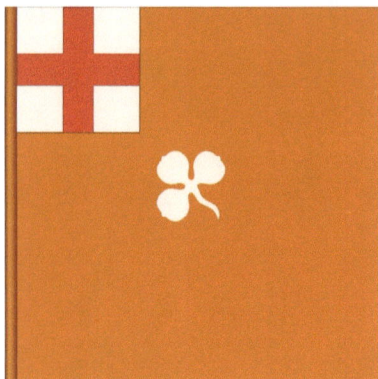

TB31. The Orange London Trayned Bands
Regiment
Major's colour 1643

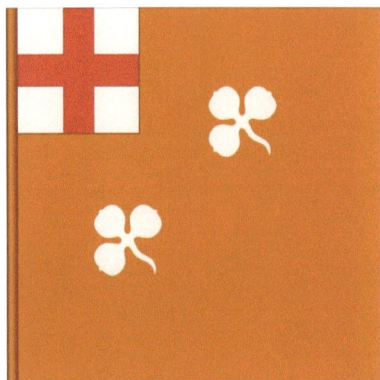

TB32. The Orange London Trayned Bands
Regiment
1st Captain's colour 1643

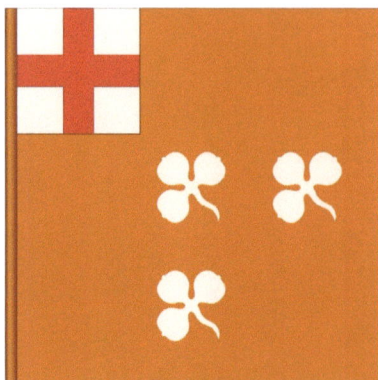

TB33. The Orange London Trayned Bands
Regiment
2nd Captain's colour 1643

TB34. The Orange London Trayned Bands
Regiment
3rd Captain's colour 1643

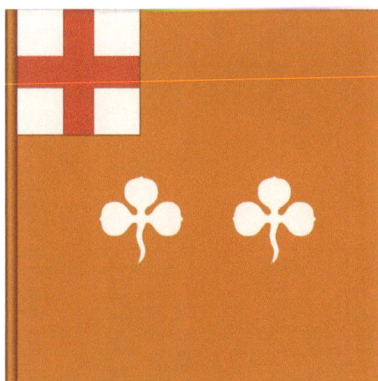

TB35. The Orange London Trayned Bands
Regiment
1st Captain's (Alternate) colour 1643

TB36. The Orange London Trayned Bands
Regiment
2nd Captain's (Alternate) colour 1643

TB37. The Orange London Trayned Bands
Regiment
3rd Captain's (Alternate) colour 1643

TB38. The Greene London Trayned Bands
Regiment
Colonel and Lt Colonel's colour 1643

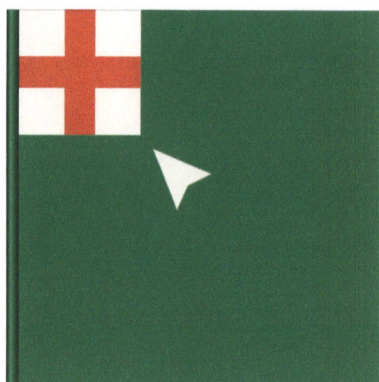

TB39. The Greene London Trayned Bands
Regiment
Major's colour 1643

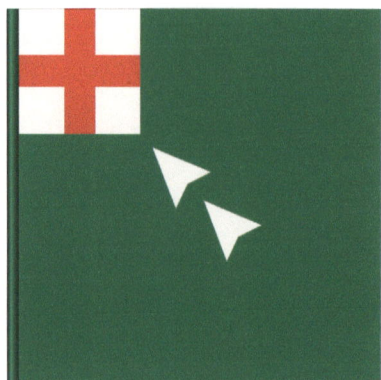

TB40. The Greene London Trayned Bands
Regiment
1st Captain's colour 1643

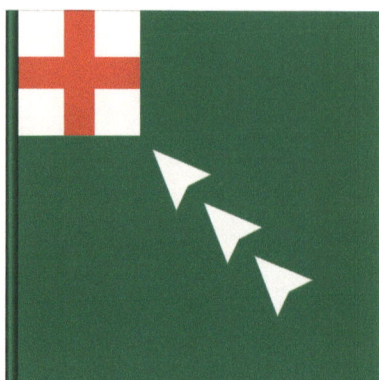

TB41. The Greene London Trayned Bands
Regiment
2nd Captain's colour 1643

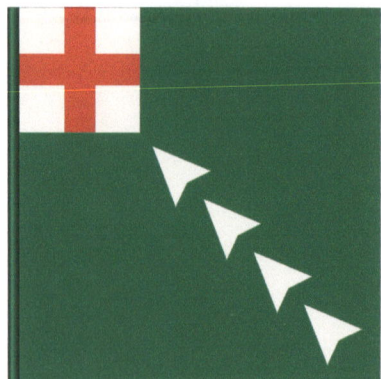

TB42. The Greene London Trayned Bands
Regiment
3rd Captain's colour 1643

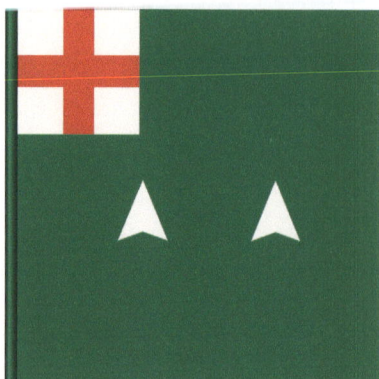

TB43. The Greene London Trayned Bands
Regiment
1st Captain's (Alternate) colour 1643

44

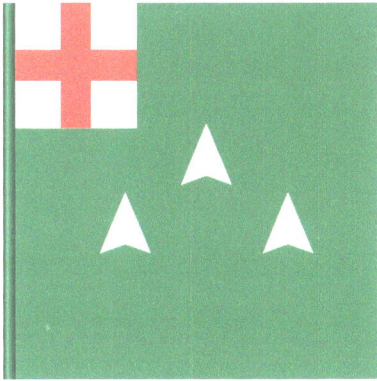

TB44. The Greene London Trayned Bands
Regiment
2nd Captain's (Alternate) colour 1643

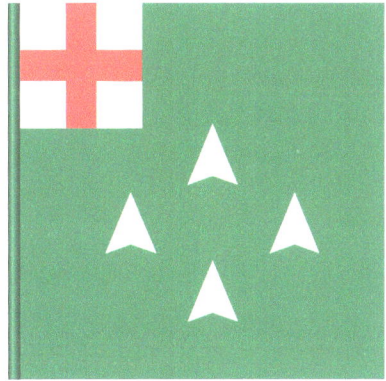

TB45. The Greene London Trayned Bands
Regiment
3rd Captain's (Alternate) colour 1643

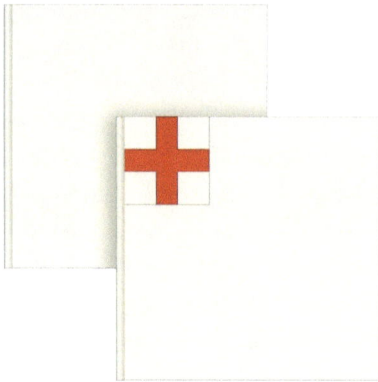

TB46. The White London Auxiliaries
Regiment
Colonel and Lt Colonel's colour 1643

TB47. The White London Auxiliaries
Regiment
Major's colour 1643

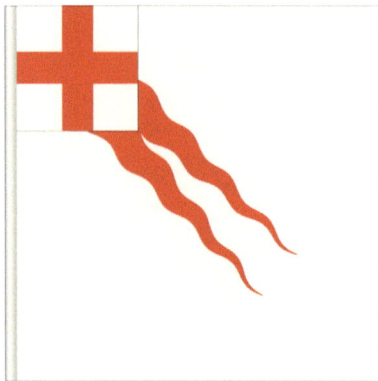

TB48. The White London Auxiliaries
Regiment
1st Captain's colour 1643

TB49. The White London Auxiliaries
Regiment
2nd Captain's colour 1643

TB50. The White London Auxiliaries
Regiment
3rd Captain's colour 1643

TB51. The White London Auxiliaries
Regiment
4th Captain's colour 1643

TB52. The Yellow London Auxiliaries
Regiment
Colonel and Lt Colonel's colour 1643

TB53. The Yellow London Auxiliaries
Regiment
Major's colour 1643

TB54. The Yellow London Auxiliaries
Regiment
1st Captain's colour 1643

TB55. The Yellow London Auxiliaries
Regiment
2nd Captain's colour 1643

TB56. The Yellow London Auxiliaries
Regiment
3rd Captain's colour 1643

TB57. The Yellow London Auxiliaries
Regiment
4th Captain's colour 1643

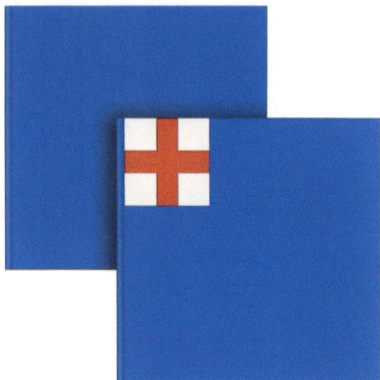

TB58. The Blew London Auxiliaries
Regiment
Colonel and Lt Colonel's colour 1643

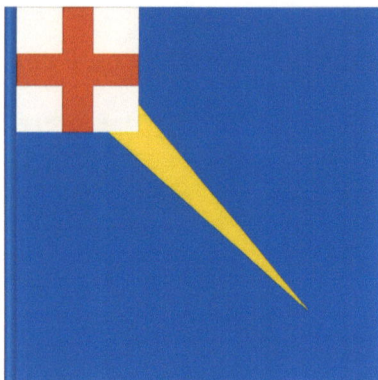

TB59. The Blew London Auxiliaries
Regiment
Major's colour 1643

TB60. The Blew London Auxiliaries
Regiment
1st Captain's colour 1643

TB61. The Blew London Auxiliaries
Regiment
2nd Captain's colour 1643

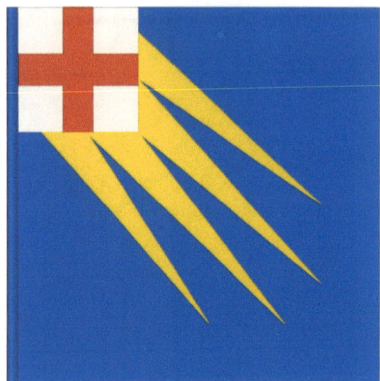

TB62. The Blew London Auxiliaries
Regiment
3rd Captain's colour 1643

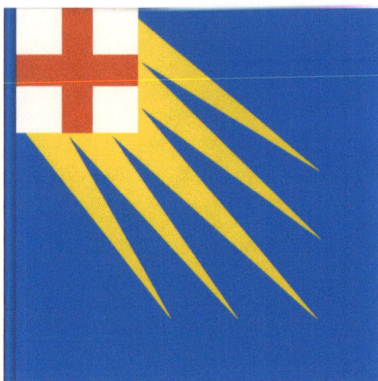

TB63. The Blew London Auxiliaries
Regiment
4th Captain's colour 1643

TB64. The Red London Auxiliaries
Regiment
Colonel and Lt Colonel's colour 1643

TB65. The Red London Auxiliaries
Regiment
Major's colour 1643

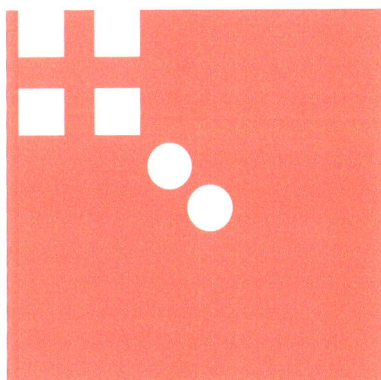

TB66. The Red London Auxiliaries
Regiment
1st Captain's colour 1643

TB67. The Red London Auxiliaries
Regiment
2nd Captain's colour 1643

TB68. The Red London Auxiliaries
Regiment
3rd Captain's colour 1643

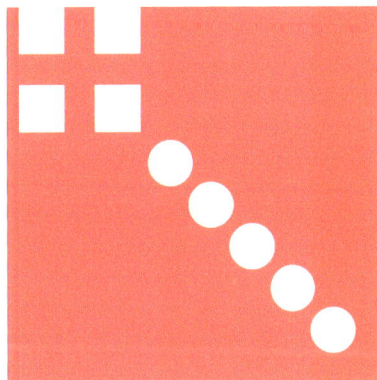

TB69. The Red London Auxiliaries
Regiment
4th Captain's colour 1643

49

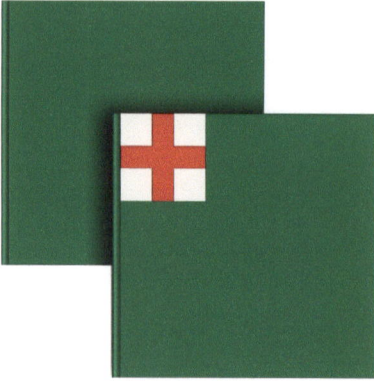

TB68. The Greene London Auxiliaries
Regiment
Colonel and Lt Colonel's colour 1643

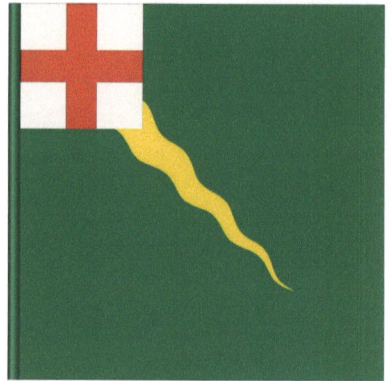

TB69. The Greene London Auxiliaries
Regiment
Major's colour 1643

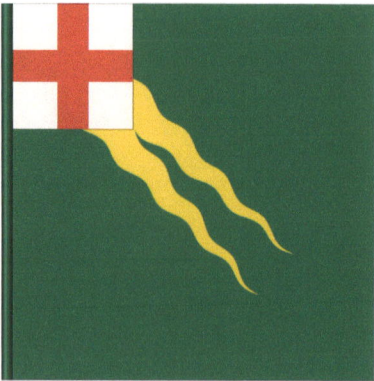

TB70. The Greene London Auxiliaries
Regiment
1st Captain's colour 1643

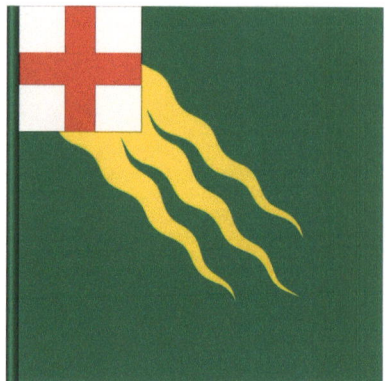

TB71. The Greene London Auxiliaries
Regiment
2nd Captain's colour 1643

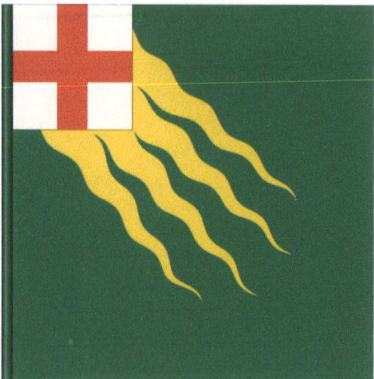

TB72. The Greene London Auxiliaries
Regiment
3rd Captain's colour 1643

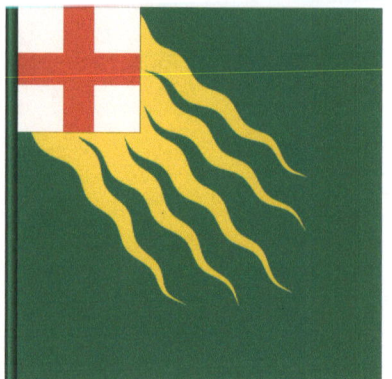

TB73. The Greene London Auxiliaries
Regiment
4th Captain's colour 1643

TB74. The Orange London Auxiliaries
Regiment
Colonel and Lt Colonel's colour 1643

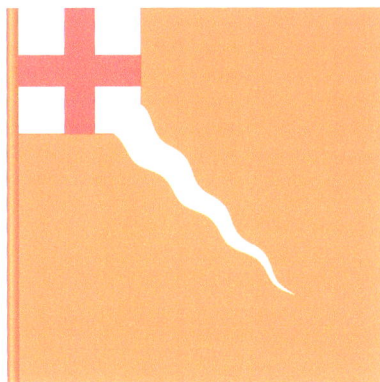

TB75. The Orange London Auxiliaries
Regiment
Major's colour 1643

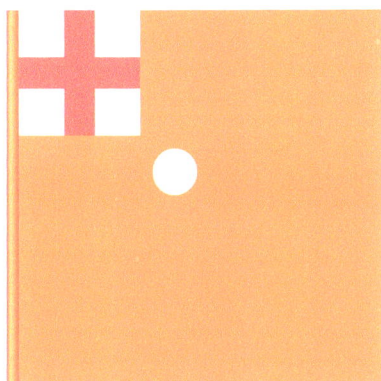

TB76. The Orange London Auxiliaries
Regiment
1st Captain's colour 1643

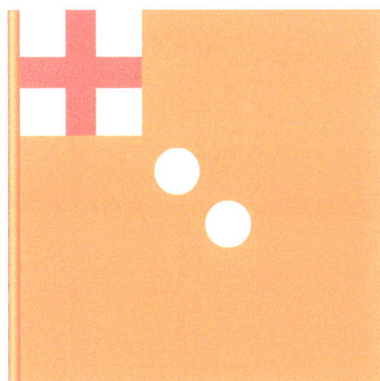

TB77. The Orange London Auxiliaries
Regiment
2nd Captain's colour 1643

TB78. The Orange London Auxiliaries
Regiment
3rd Captain's colour 1643

TB79. The Orange London Auxiliaries
Regiment
4th Captain's colour 1643

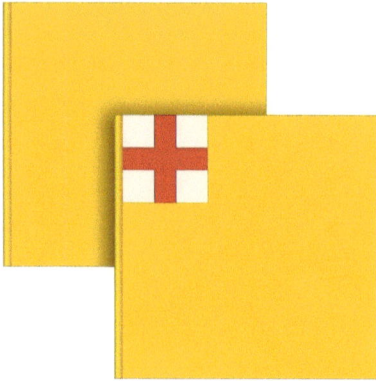

TB80. The Borough of Southwark Trayned
Band Regiment
Colonel and Lt Colonel's colour 1643

TB81. The Borough of Southwark Trayned
Band Regiment
Major's colour 1643

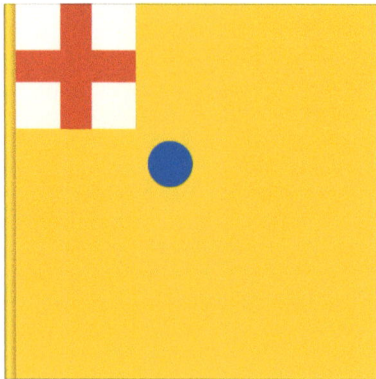

TB82. The Borough of Southwark Trayned
Band Regiment
1st Captain's colour 1643

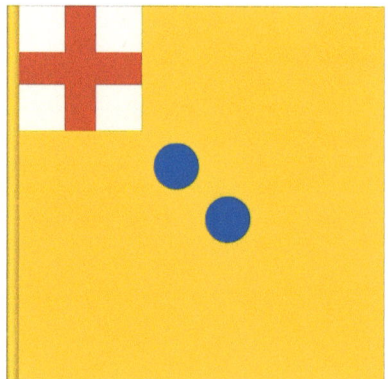

TB83. The Borough of Southwark Trayned
Band Regiment
2nd Captain's colour 1643

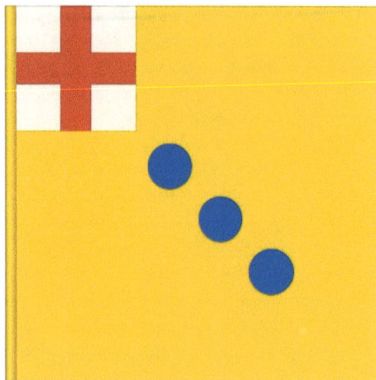

TB84. The Borough of Southwark Trayned
Band Regiment
3rd Captain's colour 1643

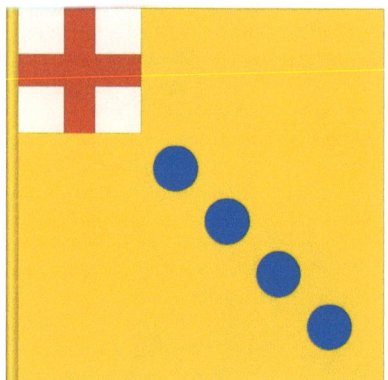

TB85. The Borough of Southwark Trayned
Band Regiment
4th Captain's colour 1643

TB86. The Borough of Southwark Trayned
Band Regiment
5th Captain's colour 1643

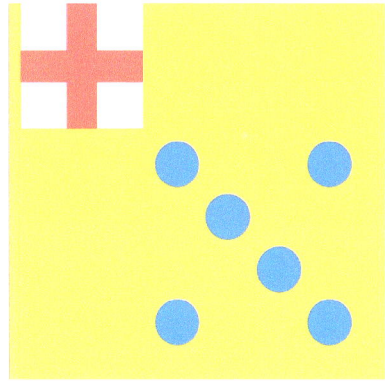

TB87. The Borough of Southwark Trayned
Band Regiment
6th Captain's colour 1643

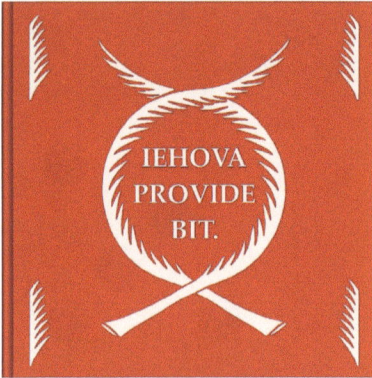

TB88. The Tower Hamlets Trayned Band
Regiment
Colonel's colour 1643

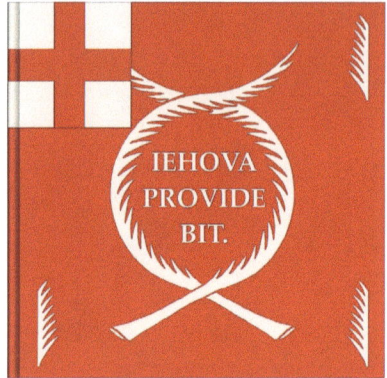

TB89. The Tower Hamlets Trayned Band
Regiment
Lt Colonel's colour 1643

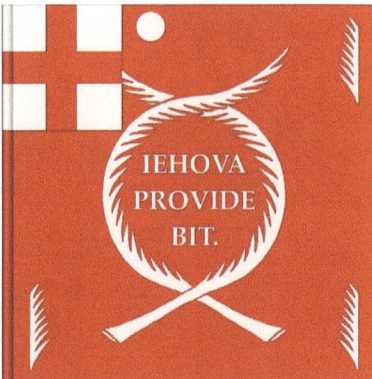

TB90. The Tower Hamlets Trayned Band
Regiment
Major's colour 1643

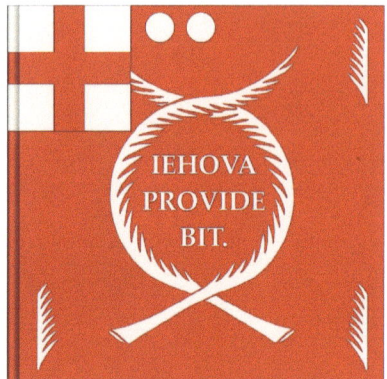

TB91. The Tower Hamlets Trayned Band
Regiment
1st Captain's colour 1643

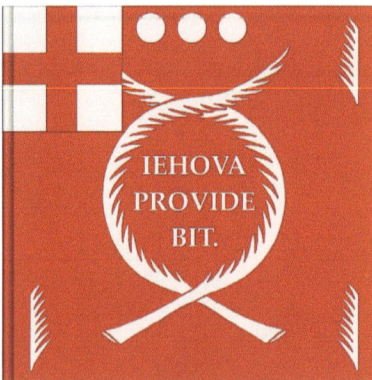

TB92. The Tower Hamlets Trayned Band
Regiment
2nd Captain's colour 1643

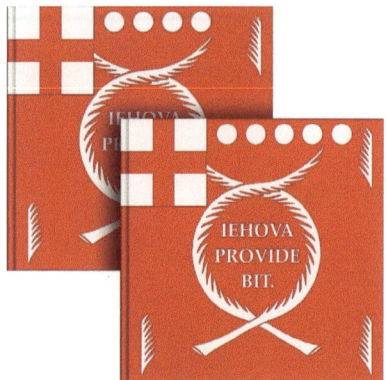

TB93. The Tower Hamlets Trayned Band
Regiment
3rd and 4th Captain's colour 1643

TB94. The Westminster Trayned Band
Regiment
Colonel and Lt Colonel's colour. 1643

TB95. The Westminster Trayned Band
Regiment
Major's colour 1643

TB96. The Westminster Trayned Band
Regiment
1st Captain's colour. 1643

TB97. The Westminster Trayned Band
Regiment
2nd Captain's colour. 1643

TB98. The Westminster Trayned Band
Regiment
3rd Captain's colour. 1643

TB99. The Westminster Trayned Band
Regiment
4th Captain's colour. 1643

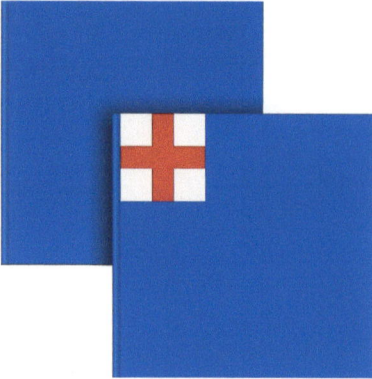

TB100. The Westminster Auxiliaries
Regiment
Colonel and Lt Colonel's colour 1643

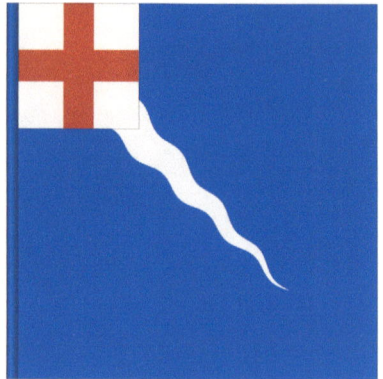

TB101. The Westminster Auxiliaries
Regiment
Major's colour 1643

TB102. The Westminster Auxiliaries
Regiment
1st Captain's colour. 1643

TB103. The Westminster Auxiliaries
Regiment
2nd Captain's colour. 1643

TB104. The Westminster Auxiliaries
Regiment
3rd Captain's colour. 1643

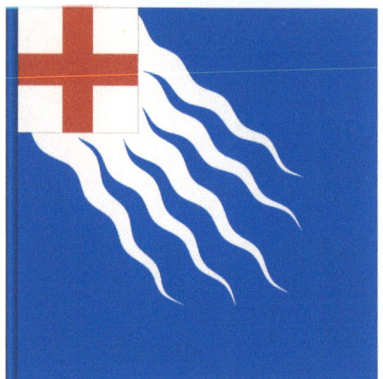

TB105. The Westminster Auxiliaries
Regiment
4th Captain's colour. 1643

Scottish Covenanter Foot Regiments

Additional Notes To Illustrations

C1. The Aberdeen Militia Regiment Colonel's white colours displaying the coat of arms for Aberdeen town.

C2-C3. Two examples from George Keith of Aden's regiment with just the distinctions as company identification. Note the lack of Covenant inscription.

C4-C6. Some of the devices displayed by Colonel John Forbes of Leslie's regiment included the crest of the Cristall family - two cherubs, a tree, table and red motto in the saltire. Also the coat of arms for Garioch (still seen quartered on the coat of arms of Aberdeen County Council) and the Forbes family stags head crest.

C7. The Colonel's flag displaying the golden cockerel crest of Sir John Innes. Other unit flags were red with a white saltire.

C8-C9. A number of flags captured at Dunbar belonging to Colonel John Lindsay of Edzell's Regiment of which just two had devices and mottos - one being the blue lion of Strathmore. C8 Small Motto 'REVIRESCO'. C9 Small motto 'O LORD DO WE IN THEE TRUST'

C10. The Colonel's flag from Richard Douglas' Regiment carries the Douglas family motto with the popular arm, sword and cloud device. Motto 'DOE OR DIE'

C11. An unknown company flag from Colonel William Stewart's regiment with the distinctive quartered red and blue field to the white saltire with the Scottish Thistle. One of a handful of surviving flags.

C12. The Colonel's flag from the Duke of Hamilton's Regiment unusually displaying just a field of ermine.

C13. The Earl of Atholl's Regiment carried flags with a red edge to the saltire.

C14-C16. At Preston in 1648 the Earl of Buccleugh's flags had a half yellow (sinister) and half white (dexter) saltire on a blue field. Individual companies were identified by the number of red stars within a green laurel.

C17. This Colonel's flag displays the gold dragon crest and motto from the Crichton family. Small motto 'god send greace'

C19-C20. The family crest of silver lion and motto appear on the Colonel's flag of the Earl of Home's Regiment (C19). Other colours had a green field with white saltire and black numerals to identify the unit. C19. Small motto 'TREV TO THE END'

C21-C22. Two examples of the Earl of Tullibardine's Regiment. The Colonel's flag carries the gold thistle of Scotland. C21 Motto around thistle 'NEMO ME IMPVNE LACESSIT'

C23-C25. The General of Artillery Regiment was formed from drafts from other units. C23 displays the red lion (Wemyss), silver bear (Forbes), black cross (Sinclair) and red heart (Douglas). C24 carries the red lion (Lt Colonel Wemyss). C25 Carries the motto and star (mullet) emblem of the Murrays of Sterling.

C27-C28. The Lord Balfour of Burleigh, colonel's flag depicted a maiden and scroll and motto 'OMNE SOLVM FORTI PATRIA'. Other units flags were black with a white saltire but with no company distinguishing markings.

C29. The Colonel's flag from Lord Balmerino's Regiment with his golden dove and snake crest and small motto 'PRVDENTIA FRAVDIS NESCIA'

C30. The stork and gold stone emblem are derived from the Cranston crest on this Regimental flag. Small motto 'VIGILANDO'

C31-C32. Lord Bargany's Regiment used red stars within a laurel to identify the captain's units.

C33-C34. The Colonel's flag displays the thunderbolt and motto of the Carnegie family. Note the mirror writing on the Covenant inscription. The other regimental colours were blue with white saltire. C33 Small motto 'dread god'. C34 Small motto 'VIRTVTE HONOR'

C35. The Colonel's flag from Lord Coupar's Regiment carries the Coupar family stag and acorn tree crest and motto 'SVB VMBRA PROFEGE'.

C37. Master of Yester's Regiment displays the silver Goat of Tweeddale surrounded by a wreath.

C38-C45. An almost complete set of flags from Sgt-Major-General Colin Pitscottie's Regiment using the heraldic cadency devices to identify individual companies. C38 and C39 are unknown companies (possibly Colonel and Sgt-Majors).

C46. A flag from Sir Alexander Fraser of Philorth's Firelocks. The central device is believed to be the arms of old Aberdeen although the Lilly flower heads and three fish on the pot are missing.

C47-C54 Sir Andrew Kerr of Greenhead's regiment originally used the heraldic cadency devices to identify companies. After a time however there must have been some reorganisation and additional numbers added next to the devices. The Colonel's flag displayed a small blue and white saltire above the thistle of Scotland. Note the mirror writing.

C55-C60. Sir Alexander Stewart's Regiment appeared to be using the English system of regimental company identification. The castle on the Colonel and Lt-Colonel's is from the City of Edinburgh. C55 and C56 Motto around Castle 'COVENANT FOR RELIGION KING AND KINGDOM'. C56 Small motto 'EXVRGO'

C61-C66. Another regiment using the heraldic cadency devices was that of Sir David Home of Wedderburn. However it is unclear what the crest and star with the Douglas family heart crest (C61) means. Also the starburst device (C66) meaning is unknown at this time.

C67. The Colonel's flag of Sir William Douglas of Kirkness Regiment displays the Douglas family crowned red heart. The meaning of the seven small stars is unknown. Small motto 'NEC TEMERE NEC TIMIDE'

C68-C70. The Colonels flag of Sir George Preston of Valleyfield's Regiment displays the family black unicorn with gold mane, horn and beard. On the two examples of Captains flags the meaning of the heraldic cadency devices has been re-enforced by painting small numbers next to them.

C71. One of few surviving flags of an unknown unit using the number of roses to identify each company.

C1. Aberdeen Militia Regiment
Colonel's colour 1640

C2. Colonel George Keith of Aden's
Regiment
Preston 1648

C3. Colonel George Keith of Aden's
Regiment
Preston 1648

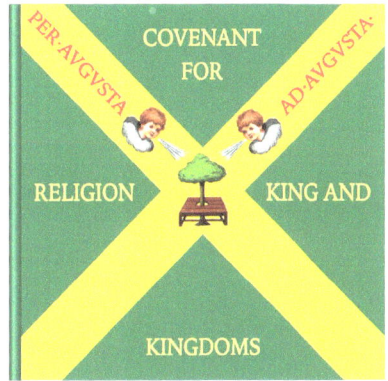

C4. Colonel John Forbes of Leslie's
Regiment.
Dunbar 1650

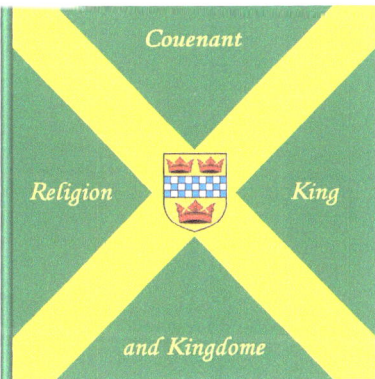

C5. Colonel John Forbes of Leslie's
Regiment
Dunbar 1650

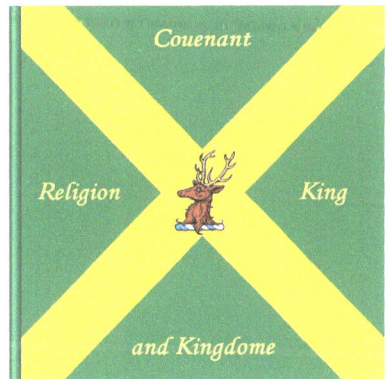

C6. Colonel John Forbes of Leslie's
Regiment
Dunbar 1650

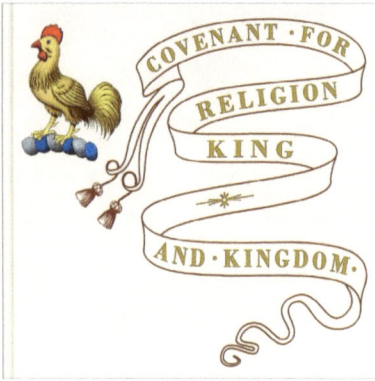

C7. Sir John Innes Regiment
Colonel's colour
Dunbar 1650

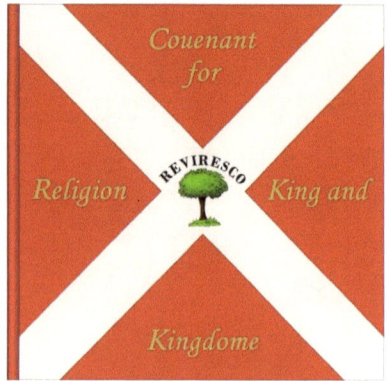

C8. Colonel John Lindsay of Edzell's
Regiment
Dunbar 1650

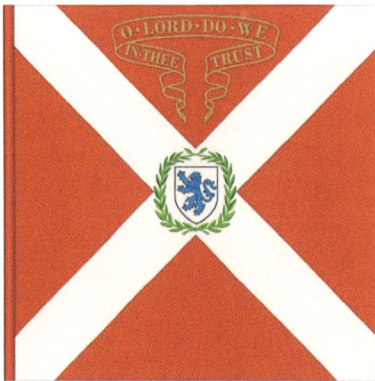

C9. Colonel John Lindsay of Edzell's
Regiment
Dunbar 1650

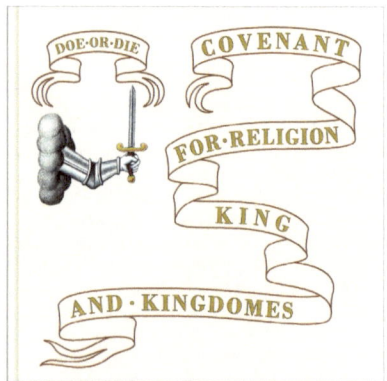

C10. Colonel Richard Douglas' Regiment
Colonel's colour. Preston 1648

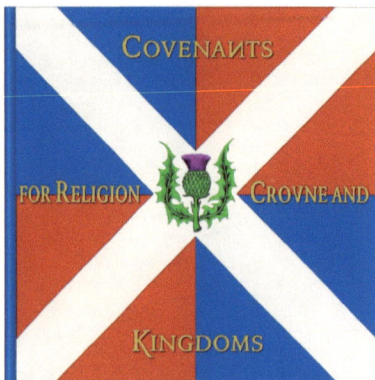

C11.. Colonel William Stewart's
Regiment
1644-1648

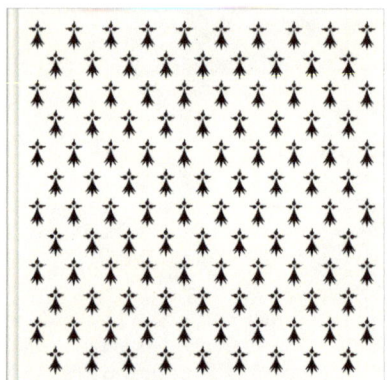

C12. Duke of Hamilton's Regiment
Colonel's colour

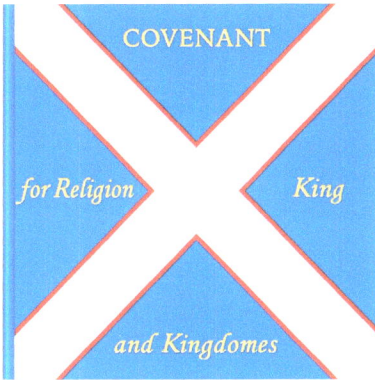

C13. Earl of Atholl's Regiment
Preston 1648

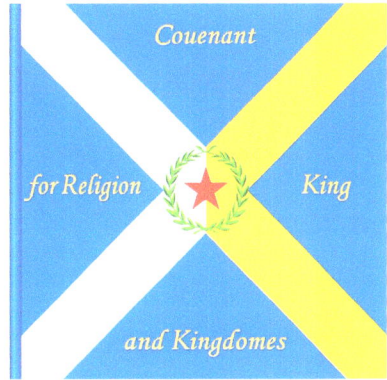

C14. Earl of Buccleugh's Regiment
1st Captain's colour. Preston 1648

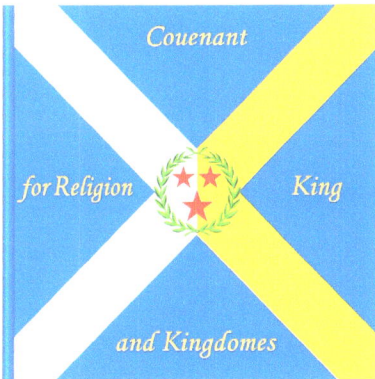

C15. Earl of Buccleugh's Regiment
3rd Captain's colour. Preston 1648

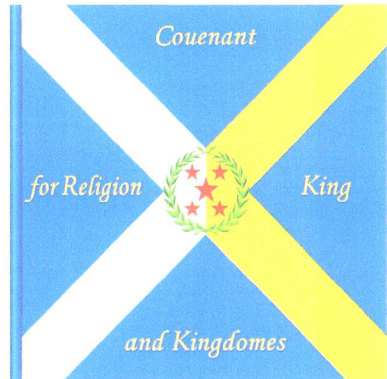

C16. Earl of Buccleugh's Regiment
5th Captain's colour. Preston 1648

C17. Earl of Dumfries' Regiment
Colonel's colour. Preston 1648

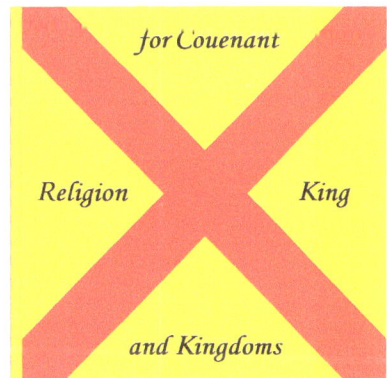

C18. Unknown Regiment
Preston 1648

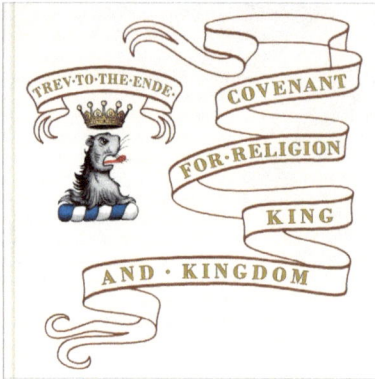

C19. Earl of Home's Regiment
Colonel's colour.
Preston 1648

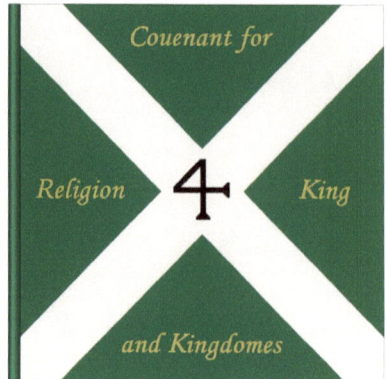

C20. Earl of Home's Regiment
4th Captain's colour.
Preston 1648

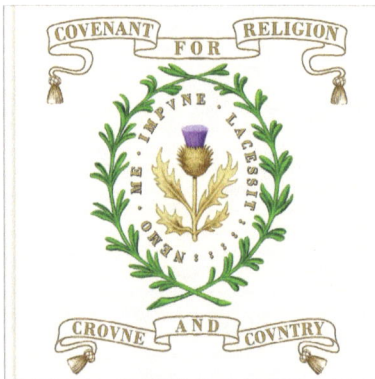

C21. Earl of Tullibardine's Regiment
Colonel's colour.
Preston 1648

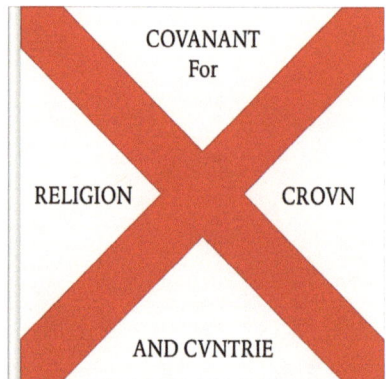

C22. Earl of Tullibardine Regiment
Preston 1648

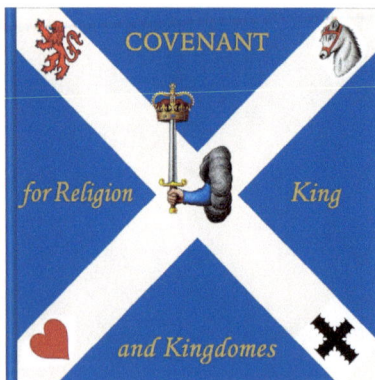

C23. General of Artillery Regiment
Colonel's colour ?
Dunbar 1650

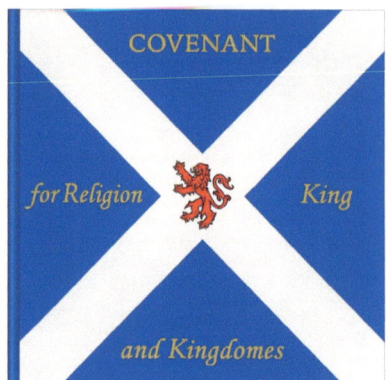

C24. General of Artillery Regiment
Lt Colonel Wemyss' colour.
Dunbar 1650

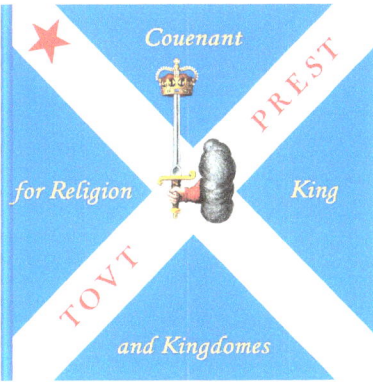

C25. General of Artillery Regiment
Dunbar 1650

C26. Levn's Lifeguard Regiment
c.1644

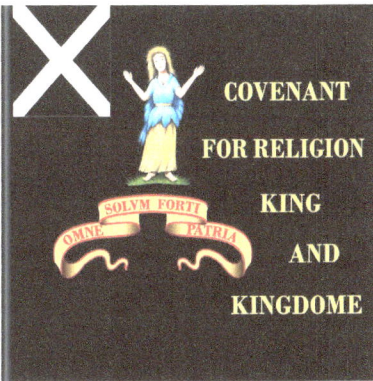

C27. Lord Balfour of Burleigh's Regiment
Colonel's colour. Dunbar 1650

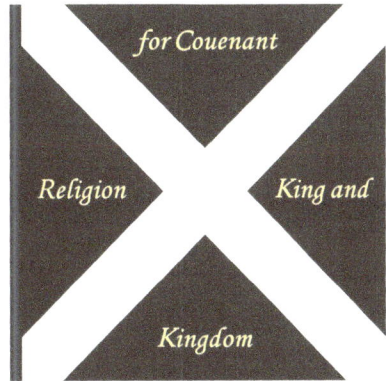

C28. Lord Balfour of Burleigh's Regiment
Dunbar 1650

C29. Lord Balmerino's Regiment
Colonel's colour. Dunbar 1650

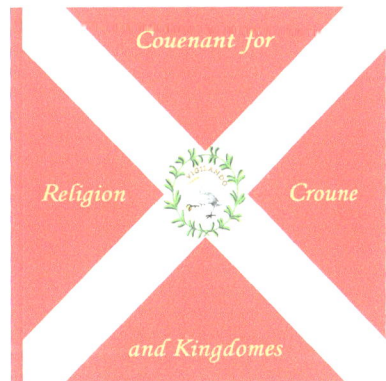

C30. Lord Cranston's Regiment
Preston 1648

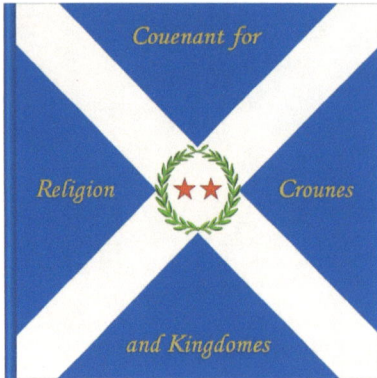

C31. Lord Bargany's Regiment
2nd Captains colour

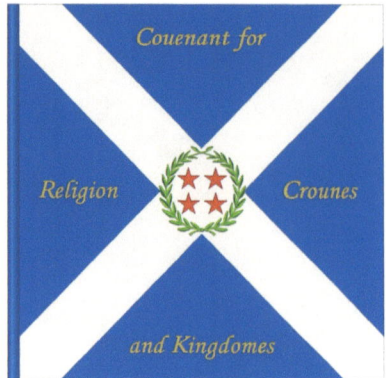

C32. Lord Bargany's Regiment
4th Captains colour

C33. Lord Carnegie's Regiment
Colonel's colour. Preston 1648

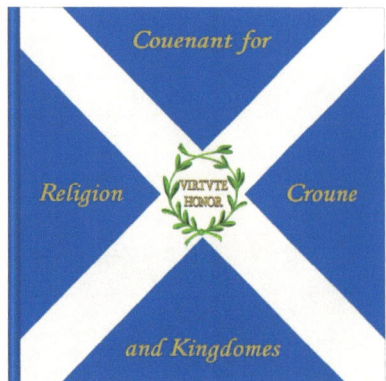

C34. Lord Carnegie's Regiment
Preston 1648

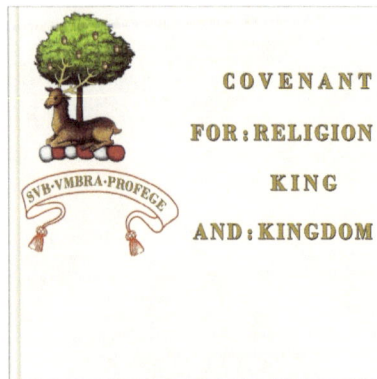

C35. Lord Coupar's Regiment
Colonel's colour

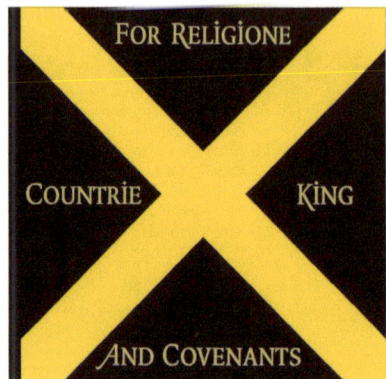

C36. Marquis of Argyll's Regiment
Preston 1648

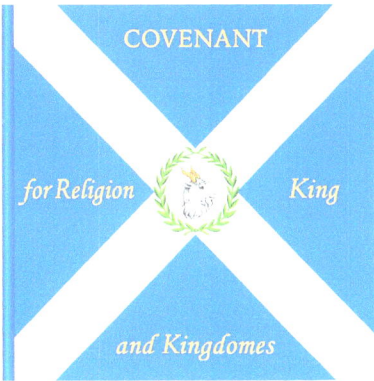
C37. Master of Yester's Regiment
Preston 1648

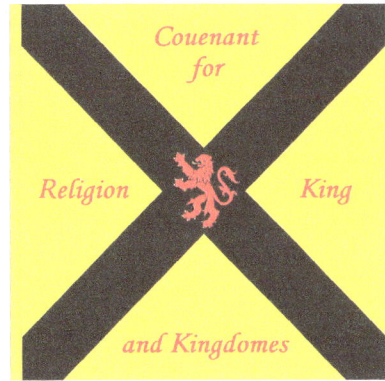
C38. Sgt-Major-General Colin Pitscottie's
Regiment
Colonel's colour? Dunbar 1650

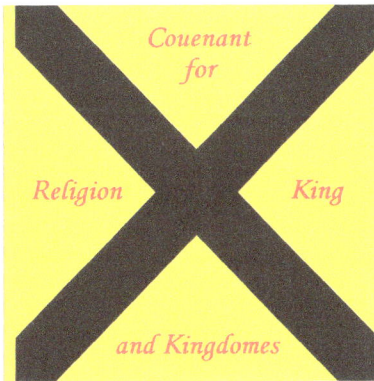
C39. Sgt-Major-General Colin Pitscottie's
Regiment
Unidentified colour. Dunbar 1650

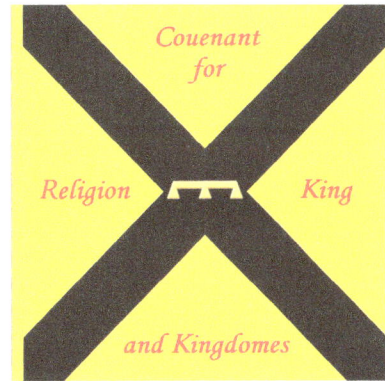
C40. Sgt-Major-General Colin Pitscottie's
Regiment.
1st Captains colour. Dunbar 1650

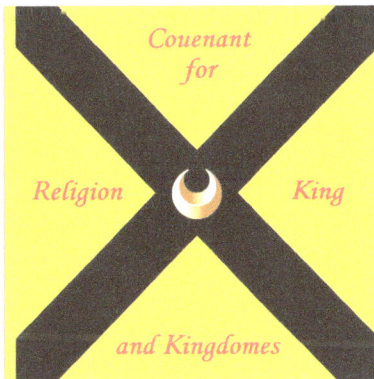
C41. Sgt-Major-General Colin Pitscottie's
Regiment.
2nd Captains colour. Dunbar 1650

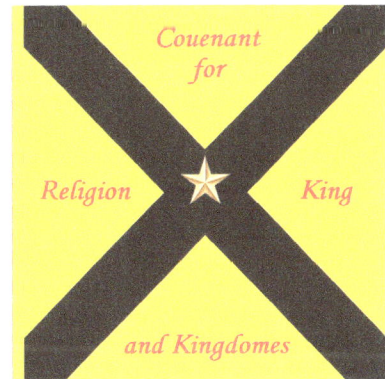
C42. Sgt-Major-General Colin Pitscottie's
Regiment.
3rd Captains colour. Dunbar 1650

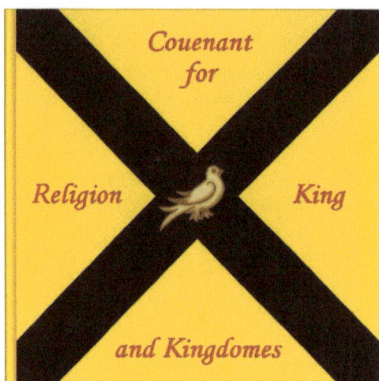

C43. Sgt-Major-General Colin Pitscottie's
Regiment.
4th Captains colour. Dunbar 1650

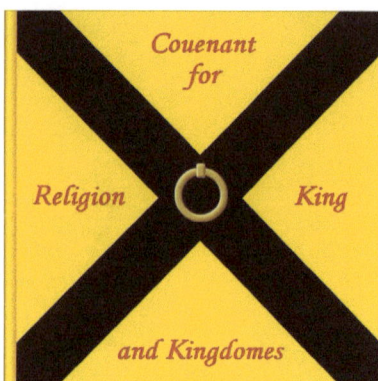

C44. Sgt-Major-General Colin Pitscottie's
Regiment.
5th Captains colour. Dunbar 1650

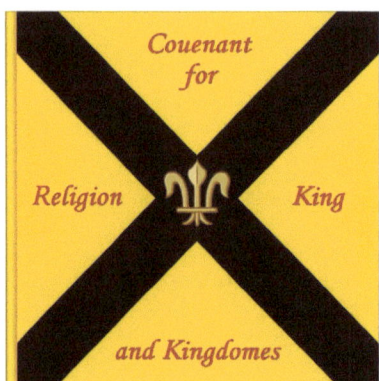

C45. Sgt-Major-General Colin Pitscottie's
Regiment.
6th Captains colour. Dunbar 1650

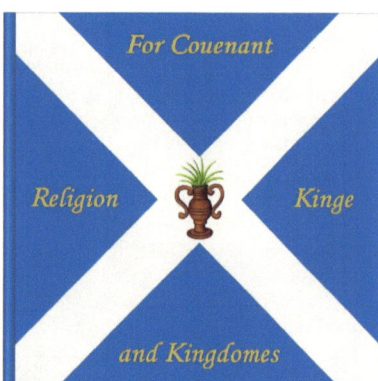

C46. Sir Alexander Fraser of Philorth's
Firelocks
1648

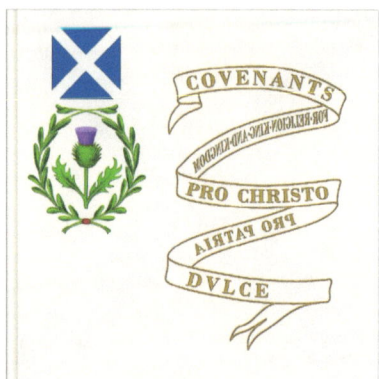

C47. Sir Andrew Kerr of Greenhead's
Regiment
Colonel's colour. Dunbar 1650

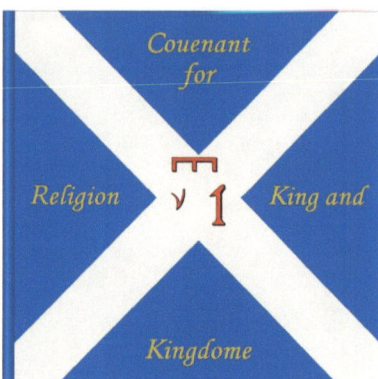

C48. Sir Andrew Kerr of Greenhead's
Regiment
Dunbar 1650

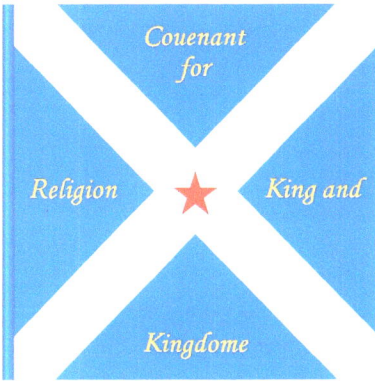

C49. Sir Andrew Kerr of Greenhead's
Regiment
Dunbar 1650

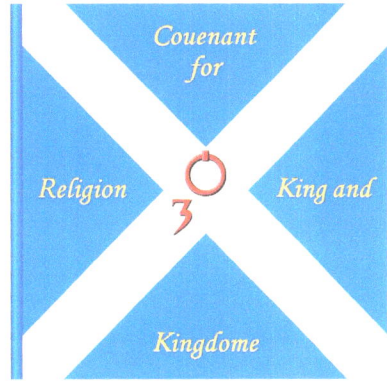

C50. Sir Andrew Kerr of Greenhead's
Regiment
Dunbar 1650

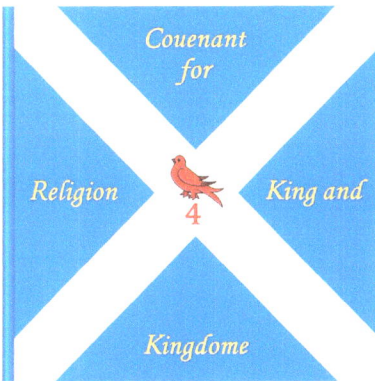

C51. Sir Andrew Kerr of Greenhead's
Regiment
Dunbar 1650

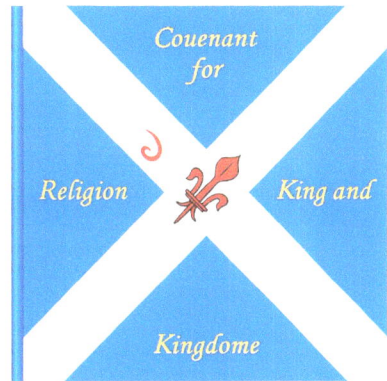

C52. Sir Andrew Kerr of Greenhead's
Regiment
Dunbar 1650

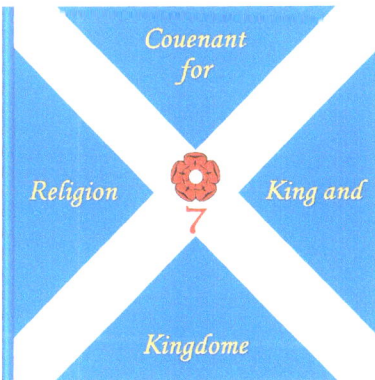

C53. Sir Andrew Kerr of Greenhead's
Regiment
Dunbar 1650

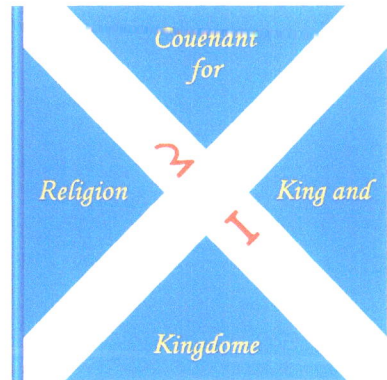

C54. Sir Andrew Kerr of Greenhead's
Regiment
Dunbar 1650

C55. Sir Alexander Stewart's Regiment
Colonel's colour
Dunbar 1650

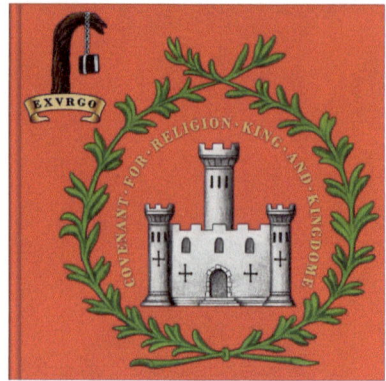

C56. Sir Alexander Stewart's Regiment
Lt Colonel's colour.
Dunbar 1650

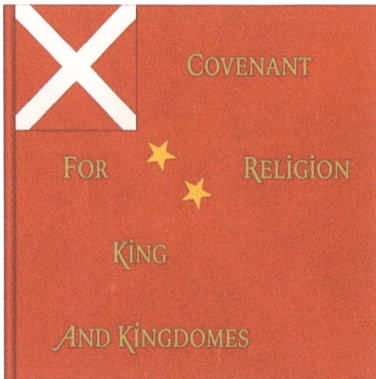

C57. Sir Alexander Stewart's Regiment
2nd Captains colour. Dunbar 1650

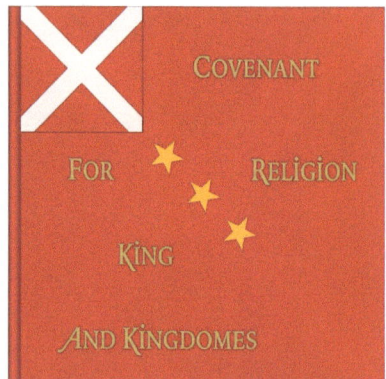

C58. Sir Alexander Stewart's Regiment
3rd Captains colour. Dunbar 1650

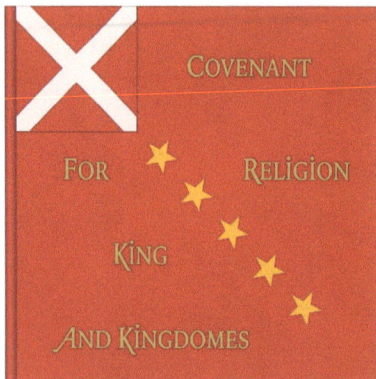

C59. Sir Alexander Stewart's Regiment
5th Captains colour. Dunbar 1650

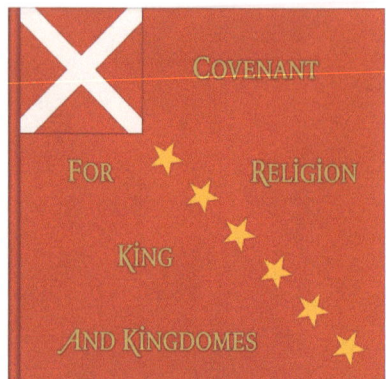

C60. Sir Alexander Stewart's Regiment
6th Captains colour. Dunbar 1650

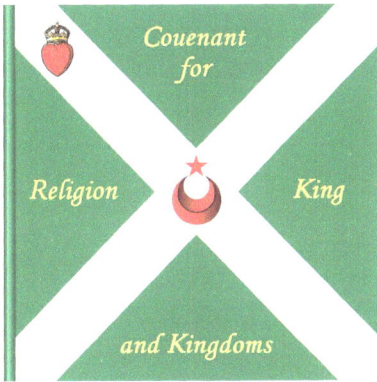

C61. Sir David Home of Wedderburn's
Regiment
Unknown colour. Dunbar 1650

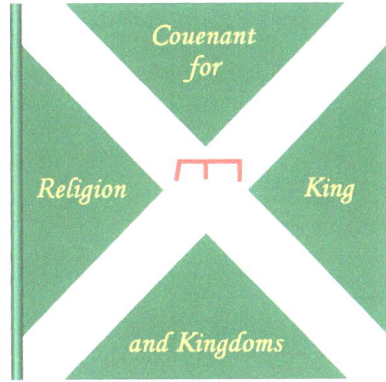

C62. Sir David Home of Wedderburn's
Regiment
1st Captains colour. Dunbar 1650

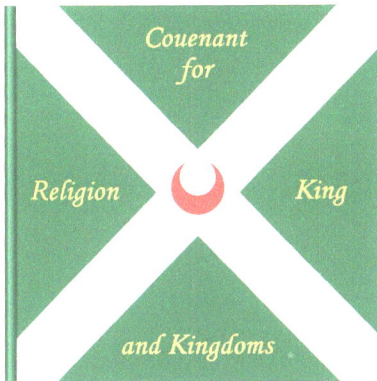

C63. Sir David Home of Wedderburn's
Regiment
2nd Captains colour. Dunbar 1650

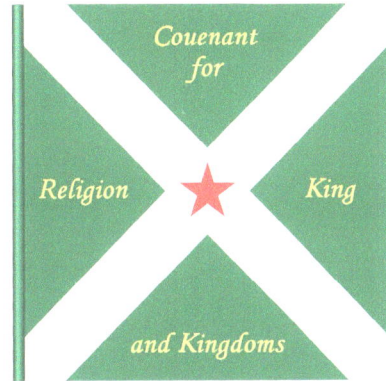

C64. Sir David Home of Wedderburn's
Regiment
3rd Captains colour. Dunbar 1650

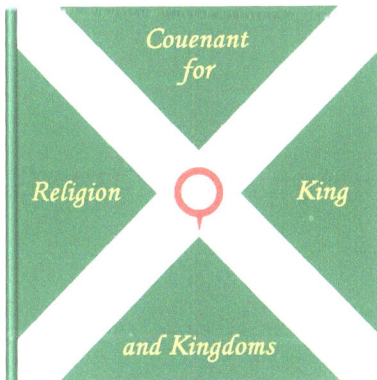

C65. Sir David Home of Wedderburn's
Regiment
5th Captains colour. Dunbar 1650

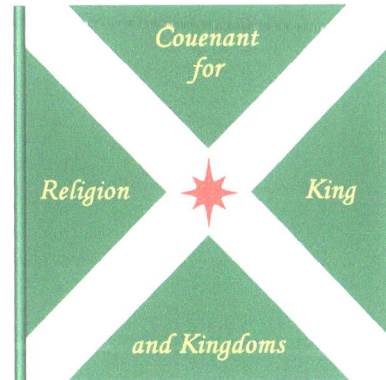

C66. Sir David Home of Wedderburn's
Regiment
Unknown colour. Dunbar 1650

C67. Sir William Douglas of Kirkness
Regiment.
Colonel's colour. Dunbar 1650

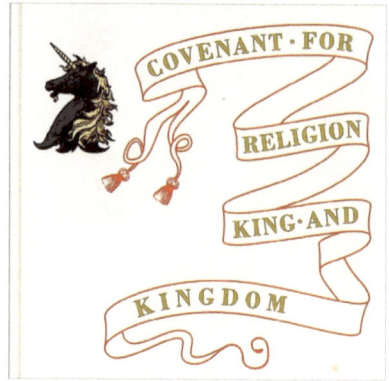

C68. Sir George Preston of Valleyfield's
Regiment.
Colonel's colour. Dunbar 1650

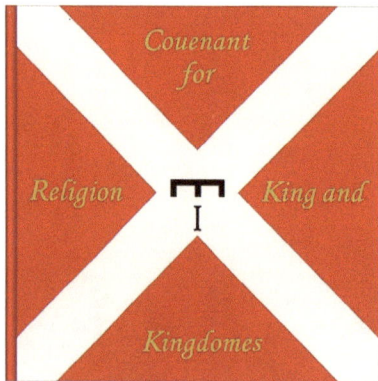

C69. Sir George Preston of Valleyfield's
Regiment.
1st Captains colour. Dunbar 1650

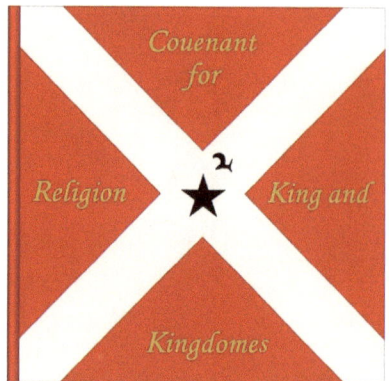

C70. Sir George Preston of Valleyfield's
Regiment.
2nd Captains colour. Dunbar 1650

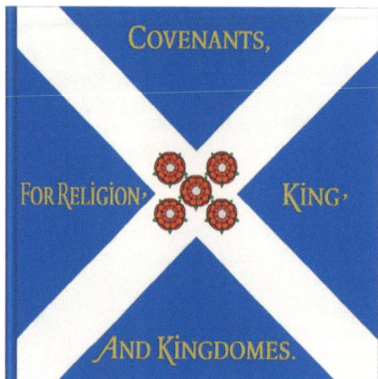

C71. Unknown Regiment
5th Captains colour?

NOTES

NOTES

-